THE

BY: LESLIE

O
T
H
E
R
S
I
D
E

S
M
I
T
H

the otherside
wriettn by leslie smith
isbn:978-1-4116-9611-2

from the
author
leslie
smith.for
informatio
n on this
title and
other
works by
this author
you can
reach him
at
richard_s
mith182@
yahoo.co
m
thank you
for
purchasin
g this
book and i
hope it
provides
hours of
reading
enjoyment

sincerely

lelsie

smith

I DEDICATE THIS BOOK TO MY FATHER, THE MOLE MAN,FOR HIS BELATED BIRTHDAY PRESENT. WITHOUT HIM IN MY LIFE I WOULD HAVE NEVER BECAME THE MAN I AM TODAY AND I AM PROUD TO CALL HIM MY DAD.
HAPPY BIRTHDAY MOLE

AND TO MY MOTHER WHO HAS ALWAYS BEEN THERE FOR ME NO MATTER HOW MUCH TROUBLE I GOT INTO SHE WAS ALWAYS THERE AND TOOK MY SIDE.

AND TO ALL THE LADIES WHO HAVE HELPED SHAPE MY LIFE AND TO THEM I NEVER REGRET ONE MOMENT I HAVE SPENT WITH ANY OF YOU AND KNOW THAT YOU HAVE SHAPED MY LIFE INTO A BETTER MORE UNDERSTANDING MAN.

LESLIE SMITH

TABLE OF CONTENTS

Chapter 1

The Beginning of the End

AS THE 6:30 TRAIN PULLED INTO THE PORT HELIO STATION I STARED OUT THE WINDOW LOOKING FOR FAMILIAR FACES AS WE PULLED INTO THE DEPOT. I KNEW THERE WAS NOONE THERE TO MEET ME THERE. I WAS ALONE AND I HAD BEEN ALONE FOR 3 YEARS NOW SINCE SHE LEFT. SHE LEFT NO NOTE NO WARNING JUST UP AND LEFT MY LIFE AS QUICKLY AS SHE WALKED IN. I REMEMBER THAT NIGHT AS IF IT WAS YESTERDAY. I WAS AT A FRIENDS BIRTHDAY PARTY WHEN I SAW HER THERE. IT WAS LOVE AT FIRST SIGHT. SHE WAS SO BEAUTIFUL. HER EYES MET MINE AND THE CONNECTION WAS MADE. IT WAS LIKE THE

BOOK WAS UNFOLDING RIGHT IN FRONT OF ME. I KNEW WHAT WAS COMING BUT I HAD NO IDEA. I MINGLED IN THE CROWD OF FIFTY OR SO FRIENDS AND GUEST BUT MY EYES SEEMED TO FOLLOW WHERE EVER SHE WENT EVEN WHEN I WAS IN ANOTHER ROOM. HANGING OUT WITH MY FRIENDS I FED MY EGO BY SHAKING THERE HANDS, AND SHOWING OFF MY POPULARITY IN THE CROWD HOPING SHE WOULD NOTICE. I SAW HERE EYES FOLLOWING ME AROUND THE ROOM AS I ENTERED; AT THAT MOMENT I KNEW SHE WAS MINE. I DANCED WITH OTHER LADIES TO CREATE SOME KIND OF URGENCY IN HER TO MAKE THE FIRST MOVE. SHE NEVER DID. I SAT THERE WONDERING WHAT ELSE I COULD DO TO MAKE HER MAKE THE MOVE FOR I DID NOT HAVE THE COURAGE TO DO SO BUT AS USUAL I FOUND SOME IN A BOTTLE THAT WOULD LATER CHANGE MY LIFE FOR THE NEXT THREE YEARS. AS I DRANK THE SPIRITS I FELT THE FALSE COURAGE BUILD TO THE POINT WHERE I COULD

ASK THE PRESIDENT FOR A DOLLAR ON THE STREET. FINALLY I FELT I WAS READY AND I MADE MY MOVE BUT INSTEAD OF SAYING A WORD I REACHED OUT AND GRABBED HER HAND AND PULLED HER OFF THE STEPS SHE WAS SITTING ON AND ASKED HER TO DANCE. SHE SAID YES. WE DANCED FOR A COUPLE OF SONGS AND I ASKED HER TO SIT WITH ME BY THE DOOR OF THE GARAGE WHERE THE MAKESHIFT DANCE FLOOR WAS MADE. THE AIR WAS HUMID AND IT WAS SO WARM OUTSIDE I FELT THAT BY SITTING THERE WOULD COOL ME AND HER DOWN. WE TALKED FOR A WHILE AND I DO NOT RECALL ABOUT WHAT. I BELIEVE WE JUST ASKED QUESTIONS ABOUT OURSELVES AND GAVE THE BEST ANSWERS WE COULD THINK OF AS IF WE WERE TRYING TO SELL OURSELVES LIKE A HIGH PRESSURE SALESMAN AT A FAILING CARLOT. THROWING OUT ANYTHING WE COULD THINK OF HOPING THE OTHER WOULD BITE HOOK LINE AND SINKER.

WHAT EVER I WAS A SAYING SEEMED TO BE WORKING. THE WORDS FLEW LIKE WINE AND AT THE END OF THE NIGHT I WAS STANDING BY MY CAR KISSING HER BEFORE SHE WENT HOME. IT WAS THE SWEETEST THING I HAVE EVER KNOWN. IT WAS AS IF I WAS KISSING 2 ROSE PEDALS THAT WERE MOIST WITH DEW AND THE AROMA OF HER PERFUME MATCHED THE OCCASION. IT WAS AS IF THERE WERE A THOUSAND JIGSAW PIECES BUT EVERY TIME I PICKED ONE UP I KNEW RIGHT WHERE IT WENT AND IT FIT JUST RIGHT. TILL FINALLY A BIGGER PICTURE WOULD BE REVEALED. BUT IT WAS ONLY OF MANY PICTURES WHICH WOULD MAKE A MUCH BIGGER PICTURE THAN I EVER WOULD IMAGINE. SOMETIMES I WISH I COULD HAVE BEEN MISSING A PIECE AND MAYBE ALL THIS PAIN WOULD HAVE BEEN AVOIDED. YES THIS WILL END BADLY OR WILL IT? I'LL LEAVE THAT UP TO THE FOLLOWING CHAPTERS AND YOUR JUDGEMENT.

WELL BACK TO THE STORY AT HAND. THE RIDE HOME WAS A SHORT ONE I ONLY LIVED A FEW MILES AWAY BUT THOUGHTS FILLED MY MIND ALL THE WAY HOME AND THEN AS I UNDRESSED AND CRAWLED INTO BED. I SET MY ALARM CLOCK, BUT THERE WOULD BE NO SLEEP TONIGHT. SHE FILLED MY HEAD AS IF SHE WERE A GHOST IN THE NIGHT SPEAKING TO ME. I THOUGHT OF OUR FIRST DATES, I THOUGHT OF OUR WEDDING, I THOUGHT OF OUR CHILDREN AND GRANDCHILDREN. I EVEN THOUGHT OF THE DOUBLE HEADSTONE WHICH BORE MY AND HER NAMES. IT WAS AS IF GOD HAD CHOSEN HER JUST FOR ME. OH HOW I HAD WAITED FOR HER, EVEN PRAYED FOR HER TO COME AND NOW SHE WAS HERE. THE REST WAS UP TO ME. THIS WAS A MATCH MADE IN HEAVEN. THE BLISS I FELT AS SHE FILLED MY SLEEP AND AS THE ALARM SOUNDED I SPRANG UP IN A HURRY. I RACED OFF TO WORK THINKING OF HER. I

KNEW I COULD NOT CALL TO EARLY BUT I DID ANYWAY AND TO MY SURPRISE SHE WAS AWAKE AND I THINK SHE WAS WAITING ON ME. MY MOTHERS BIRTHDAY WAS THAT DAY AND LATER THAT EVENING I HAD TO GOTO HER PARTY IN NC ALMOST 2 HOURS AWAY. BUT OH GOD I WANTED TO SEE HER TONIGHT. I ALMOST CANCELLED BUT I COULD NOT MY MOMS HEART WOULD BE BROKEN. WE DID NOT SEE HER THAT OFTEN SINCE THE MOVE AND THIS WAS HER SPECIAL DAY. SO I ASKED HER. WOULD YOU LIKE TO GO WITH ME TONIGHT TO A BIRTHDAY PARTY? SHE SAID NO. SHE HAD SOME THINGS TO DO THAT DAY BUT SHE SAID TO CALL HER AS SOON AS I GOT HOME. I COULD NOT WAIT I RUSHED TO THE PARTY CRAMMED DOWN SOME CAKE, DRANK A FEW BEERS SAID A COUPLE OF I LOVE YOUS AND I WAS ON THE WAY HOME. THE BEGGED NOT TO RUSH OFF BUT I USED WORK AS AN EXCUSE. TO BE HONEST I DO NOT EVEN THINK I HAD TO WORK

THE NEXT DAY. THIS BEAUTIFUL LADY HAD TOTALLY STOLEN MY HEART. I FUMBLED RUSHING TO GET MY KEY IN THE DOOR THAT JUST DID NOT SEEM TO FIT. IT WAS LIKE A HORROR MOVIE WHERE THE PERSON BEING CHASED BY THE MONSTER STRUGGLES TO UNLOCK A DOOR TO GET TO SAFETY. THAT WAS ME. MY SAFETY WAS GRABBING THAT PHONE AND HEARING HER SWEET VOICE ON THE OTHER END OF THE LINE. RING ONCE, TWICE, THREE TIMES. COME ON PICK UP THE PHONE. FINALLY SHE ANSWERED AND WE TALKED THE NIGHT AWAY. HER VOICE SOUNDING SO SWEET ON THE LINE. I WANTED TO GO THROUGH THE LINE AND HOLD HER. I TALKED TO HER ALL NIGHT. THE TIME FLEW BY SO FAST. WE TALKED ABOUT THIS AND THAT TILL I COULD BARELY HOLD MY EYES OPEN. WE MADE A DATE FOR A COUPLE OF NIGHT LATER AND THEN WE SAID OUR GOODNIGHTS I THINK I EVEN KISSED HER OVER THE PHONE. AS I LAID THERE IN MY BED I

COULD STILL HERE HER VOICE IN MY HEAD. THE NEXT COUPLE OF NIGHTS WENT BY THE SAME WAY. WE WOULD TALK FOR HOURS AND THEN FINALLY DAY FOR THE DATE CAME. THE HOURS WENT BYE SO SLOWLY. I THOUGHT THE TIME WOULD NEVER COME FOR ME TO GET IN MY CAR AND HEAD TOWARDS HER HOUSE WHICH WAS AN HOUR DRIVE FROM MINE.

I FINALLY GOT OFF WORK AND PULLED INTO MY DRIVE. I WENT STRAIGHT TO THE SHOWER WASHING MATICUOSLY EVERY INCH OF MY BODY MAKING SURE NOT TO MISS A SPOT. I JUMPED OUT AND DRIED OFF AND GRABBED MY TOOTHPASTE AND BRUSH. I BRUSHED MY TEETH AND GRABBED MY DEODORANT. I GRABBED MY BEST SHIRT AND BEST PAIR OF PANTS I HAD. I STRETCHED OUT THE IRONING BOARD AND WENT TO WORK. THERE WAS NOT A SINGLE WRINKLE ON ANYTHING WHEN I WAS DONE. TONIGHT

DESERVED PERFECTION AND PERFECTION IS WHAT IT WOULD GET. I SLOWLY DRESSED AS IF NOT TO WRINKLE THE CLOTHES I WAS PUTTING ON. THEN I GRABBED THE GEL AND MY COMB AND STYLED MY HAIR MAKING SURE NOT ONE STRAND OF HER WAS OUT OF PLACE. I COUNTED MY MONEY AND FOLDED IT NEATLY IN MY FRONT POCKET LIKE THE RICH PEOPLE DO. I PLACED ON MY NECKLACE AND RING AND I WAS READY. THEN I LOOKED AT THE CLOCK THE DATE WAS NOT FOR ANOTHER FEW HOURS. I GOT SO EXCITED THAT I FORGOT TO WAIT FOR THE DATE. I SAT THERE IN MY RECLINER TRYING NOT TO WRINKLE MY CLOTHES. THE TICKS ON THE CLOCK WENT BY SO SLOW I THOUGHT IT WOULD NEVER BE TIME TO LEAVE. MAN THIS WOULD BE THE GREATEST NIGHT OF MY LIFE. I HAD BEEN DREAMING OF THIS NIGHT FOR DAYS SINCE I LAID EYES ON HER SOFT MILKY SKIN AND BEAUTIFUL RED HAIR. FINALLY IT WAS TIME. I GOT INTO MY TRUCK

AND RODE OFF. I TRIED TO GET THERE AS FAST AS I COULD. THOUGHTS OF HER FILLED MY HEAD AS I DROVE. THE RIDE ONLY TOOK AN HOUR BUT IT FELT LIKE THE RODE WENT ON FOR DAYS. FINALLY I WAS HERE I PULLED INTO HER DRIVE. I TOOK ONE LAST LOOK IN THE MIRROR THAT WAS ON THE BACK SIDE OF MY SUN VISOR AND STEPPED OUT OF THE TRUCK AND MADE MY WAY NERVOUSLY TO THE DOOR. I RANG THE BELL AND TRIED TO SEE THROUGH THE PEEP HOLE TO SEE HER ANSWER THE DOOR. I SEEN MOVEMENT THEN I SAW THE RED HAIR. IT WAS HER. I WAS RIGHT ON TIME AND SHE WAS OPENING THE DOOR. THE KNOB SLOWLY TURNED AND THE DOOR CREAKED OPEN. I COULD NOT WAIT FOR THIS MOMENT AND NOW THE MOMENT WAS FINALLY HERE. WOW!!!!

Chapter 2

The Date of All Dates

THE DOOR FINALLY OPENED ENOUGH FOR ME TO STEP INSIDE AND WHAT WAITED ON THE OTHER SIDE STOPPED MY HEART RIGHT IN ITS TRACK. I HAD BECOME THE DEER IN THE MIDDLE OF THE ROAD BLINDED BY THE LIGHTS OF ONCOMING TRAFFIC. LOVE HIT ME AS IF IT WERE A MACK TRUCK PLUNGING DEEP IN MY HEART. THIS WAS THE FEELING I LONGED FOR ALL MY LIFE. THIS WAS IT. I KNEW FROM THAT INSTANCE SHE WAS THE ONE FOR ME. SHE INVITED ME INSIDE. AS I WALKED IN PASSED THE COFFEE TABLE WHICH WAS POSITIONED IN FRONT OF THE COUCH IN THE MIDDLE OF THE ROOM I COULD SMELL AN AROMA COMING FROM THE SMALL APARTMENT KITCHEN WHICH

SMELLED DELIGHTFUL. SHE SAID ☐MAKE YOUR SELF AT HOME AND ILL HAVE DINNER READY IN A SECOND.@ I GRABBED THE REMOTE FROM THE COFFEE TABLE AND SURFED THE TUBE FOR ANYTHING I THOUGHT SHE MIGHT ENJOY WATCHING. I MADE SURE NOT TO MAKE ANY OF THE ORDINARY GUY MISTAKES SUCH AS FLIPPING ON A FIGHT OR A BALL GAME. I HEARD HER HOLLER FROM THE KITCHEN. DINNERS READY, AND I ROSE UP AND MADE MY WAY TO THE KITCHEN WHERE A OVERSIZED TABLE SET IN THE MIDDLE OF THE SMALL APARTMENT DINING AREA. THE FOOD LOOKED DELICIOUS. IT WAS SPREAD OUT OVER THE TABLE AS IF IT WERE SOME KIND OF FEAST AND IT WAS ALL FOR ME. MAYBE SHE FELT THE SAME WAY ABOUT ME. MAYBE I WAS HER KNIGHT IN SHINING ARMOR, HER ROMEO, HER PRINCE VALIANT COME TO WHISK HER AWAY ON MY TRUSTING STEED INTO A FERRY TALE LIFE SHE ONCE DREAMED OF AS A CHILD. HOW I WISH I

14

COULD BE THAT MAN BUT MY OLD TRUCK WAS HARDLY A TRUSTING STEED. IT BARELY GOT ME HERE TO START WITH, AND MY CLOTHES WERE OK BUT IT WAS NOT ANY KNIGHTS ARMOR ORDINARY CLOTHES. SHE WAS ABLE TO SEE THROUGH THAT MATERIAL STUFF. SHE SAW MY HEART AND MY HEART WAS AS VALIANT AND BRAVE AS ANY PRINCE OR KNIGHT'S WOULD BE. AS WE DINED WE HAD CONVERSATION OF THIS AND THAT AND FOUND OURSELVES LOST. WE TOLD STORIES OF OUR LIFE BEFORE AND FUNNY THINGS THAT WE HAD ENCOUNTERED IN THE CRUEL DATING WORLD. EVERYTHING JUST CLICKED TOGETHER. IT WAS GREAT I HOPED THE DATE WOULD NEVER END. I JUDGED MY WORDS BEFORE I SAID THEM SO I WOULD NOT OFFEND HER. I CAUTIOUSLY CHEWED, NOT TAKING BITES THAT WERE TOO BIG. I NOTICED THE SAME CAUTIOUSNESS IN HER AS WELL. WE FINALLY FINISHED OUR MEAL AND WE MADE OUR WAY TO THE COUCH. I SAT TOWARDS THE

FARTHEST END TO SEE HOW CLOSE SHE WOULD SIT TO ME AND HOW MUCH SHE TRUSTED ME. SHE SAT RIGHT BESIDE ME AND LAID BACK ONTO MY SHOULDER. SHE FELT VERY COMFORTABLE WITH ME. IT WAS AS IF WE WERE TOGETHER FOR YEARS. WE WATCHED A MOVIE AND SHE YAWNED AS IF TO HINT SHE WAS TIRED SO I TOLD HER I WOULD LEAVE IF SHE WOULD LIKE ME TOO. INSTEAD SHE INVITED ME UP TO HER ROOM TO LIE DOWN WITH HER. I DID NOT HESITATE. I ACTUALLY THINK I BEAT HER TO THE ROOM. AS WE LAY ON HER BED FULLY CLOTHED WE BEGAN TO KISS STARTING OFF SLOWLY AND THEN MORE AND MORE PASSIONATELY. WE GOT LOST IN THE MOMENT AND BEFORE WE KNEW IT WE WERE MAKING THE SWEETEST LOVE I EVER MADE IN MY LIFE AND IT WAS NOT PORNO SEX. THIS WAS LOVE. WE MADE LOVE LIKE WE WERE IN A NINETEEN FIFTIES MOVIE. I THINK I ACTUALLY SAW THE FIREWORKS. I PERFORMED TO MINE

AND PAST HER EXPECTATIONS. IT WAS THE SWEETEST THING I HAVE EVER KNOWN AND I'M AFRAID IT WILL BE THE ONLY TIME IN MY LIFE I WILL EVER HAVE THIS FEELING AGAIN. ALL THE NERVOUSNESS WAS GONE WITH THE SUBTLE TOUCH OF HER HANDS ON MY BODY. WE CREATED MAGIC AND WE WERE BOTH THE MAGICIANS. IT HAD TO BE LOVE. NOTHING SO BEAUTIFUL COULD EVER COME FROM ANY WHERE ELSE. THE NEXT MORNING I AWOKE TO FIND HER STARING AT ME AND I LOOKED BACK INTO HER BIG BLUE EYES. HER FLAMING RED HAIR AND MILKY WHITE SKIN SEEMED TO MAKE HER EYES GLOW LIKE A LIGHT. THE CONTRAST WAS SPECTACULAR. WE SLOWLY KISSED, I DO NOT EVEN THINK NEITHER ONE OF US MINDED THE MORNING BREATH. LOL. THIS KISS WAS JUST AS SWEET AND AS PASSIONATE AS THE NIGHT BEFORE. WE BOTH GOT UP AND JUMPED IN THE SHOWER TOGETHER .WE MADE PASSIONATE LOVE ONCE AGAIN IN THE

17

SHOWER, IT TOO WAS GREAT. MAN THIS BEAUTIFUL LADY IS WAY TOO GOOD TO BE TRUE. IT WAS UNBELIEVABLE. I WAS SO SHOCKED. GOD HAD CHOSEN ME TO BE WITH THIS BEAUTIFUL WOMAN. IF SHE TOLD ME SHE NEVER WANTED TO SEE ME AGAIN I WOULD STILL BEEN HAPPY BECAUSE I HAD BEEN WITH MY DREAM GIRL. THE ONE THING EVERY GUY DREAMED OF ALL HIS LIFE. THE GIRL HE HAD IMAGINED IN HIS MIND COUNTLESS TIMES IN HIS LIFE. SHE WAS MY CALENDER GIRL. SHE WAS MY CENTERFOLD. AS I DRESSED, GAVE HER A GOODBYE KISS, I WALKED OUT THE DOOR, AND CLIMBED INTO MY TRUCK. IT CRANKED THANK GOD AS I DROVE HOME THOUGHTS OF HER FLEW AROUND IN MY HEAD LIKE BUSY HONEY BEES TENDING THERE NEST. IT WAS GREAT. IF I HAD ANY DOUBT IN WHAT HEAVEN WAS IT WAS ELIMINATED RIGHT HERE AND NOW. THIS WAS HEAVEN.

I PULLED INTO MY BUSINESS DRIVEWAY AND WENT IN. EVERYONE WAS ASKING ABOUT MY DATE THE NIGHT BEFORE. THIS WAS TOO SPECIAL TO SHARE THIS MOMENT WAS ALL MINE. THEY ALL PRIED AND PRIED BUT I WAS GIVING UP NOTHING BUT BORING DETAILS. ⱯYEAH I WENT OVER WE ATE DINNER AND THEN I CAME HOME, IT WAS OK.@ I BUSTLED AROUND THE OFFICE TRYING TO STAY BUSY AS I COULD TO PASS THE TIME. EVERY TIME THE PHONE RANG I WAS THERE. I ANSWERED IT SO FAST NOONE IN THE OFFICE HAD A CHANCE AND IN A SALES ATMOSPHERE PHONES WERE EVERYTHING. AFTER ABOUT TEN CALLS I FINALLY HEARD THAT SWEET VOICE. AS I LISTENED TO HER VOICE IT TOOK ME BACK TO THE NIGHT BEFORE. I WAITED ON EVERY WORD TILL IT FINALLY CAME. ⱯWOULD YOU LIKE TO SEE ME AGAIN? Ɐ@YES I WOULD BUT THIS TIME IM COOKING YOU DINNER AT MY HOUSE. ⱯSHE AGREED AND WE SET A TIME AND I HUNG UP. I

19

WANTED TO TELL HER SO BAD I LOVED HER BUT WHO COULD LOVE   SOMEONE AFTER BEING WITH THEM ONE NIGHT, BUT I DID. I TRULY DID MORE THAN ANYONE OR ANYTHING I HAD EVER LOVED BEFORE. AS I WENT THROUGH THE REST OF MY DAY I THOUGHT OF HER. AS SOON AS WE CLOSED I RAN TO THE GROCERY STORE AND PICKED OUT TWO STEAKS AND BAKING POTATOES. I WOULD MAKE HER A DINNER SHE WOULD NEVER FORGET. I GOT A BOTTLE OF WINE. I KNEW VERY LITTLE ABOUT WINE SO I JUST GRABBED THE MOST EXPENSIVE BOTTLE THEY HAD. I CAN NOT EVEN REMEMBER WHAT COLOR IT WAS. ALL THAT MATTERED IS THAT THE BOTTLE WAS FANCY, COVERED WITH PRETTY FLOWERS AND SOME FAMOUS VINEYARD NAME. I GRABBED SOME FLOWERS AND OFF TO THE HOUSE I WENT. AS I GOT DINNER DONE I PUT IT OUT ON THE TABLE AS IF I WAS A WAITER AT SOME EXPENSIVE COUNTRY CLUB. I GOT OUT MY BEST GLASSES AND

PLATES. LUCKILY I HAD TWO THAT MATCHED. YOU GOTTA REMEMBER IM STILL A BACHELOR AND THIS WAS A BACHELOR PAD. SHE CAME IN AND THE DINNER WAS EXQUISITE. SHE ATE EVERY BIT LEAVING HER PLATE BARE AND DRANK THE WINE. GREAT SHE LIKED IT. I WAS WORRIED ABOUT THAT KNOWING SO LITTLE ABOUT WINE. EXPENSIVE ALCOHOL TO ME WAS A CASE OF PREMIUM BEER. LOL. WE SPENT THIS NIGHT PRETTY MUCH LIKE THE NIGHT BEFORE AND THAT IS HOW IT ALL STARTED. FROM THEN ON WE WERE TOGETHER ALL THE TIME. WE WERE IN LOVE AND WE WERE IN LOVE AND IT SHOWED. I HAD A SPRING IN MY STEP EVERY ONE NOTICED INCLUDING THE GUYS AT WORK. I DID NOT HAVE TO SAY A THING THEY ALL KNEW. THIS WAS THE START OF SOMETHING BEAUTIFUL WHICH MY EYES HAD NEVER SEEN BEFORE. A MATCH MADE IN HEAVEN.

Chapter 3

The Answer That Will Change My Life

AFTER COUNTLESS EPISODES OF SLEEP OVERS AND LONG WEEKEND GETAWAYS TOGETHER I FELT IT WAS TIME. THE TIME TO SAY aI LOVE YOU@, BUT WHAT WOULD SHE SAY IN RETURN. USUALLY WITH MOST LADIES THE NEWNESS WOULD HAVE WORE OFF BY NOW BUT SHE WAS DIFFERENT. EVERY TIME I SAW HER IT WAS LIKE THE FIRST WE EVER LAID EYES ON EACH OTHER AT THE PARTY WHERE THE SPARK IGNITED THAT NIGHT INTO A PASSIONATE FLAME. IT WAS INCREDIBLE, BUT DID SHE FEEL THE SAME. THIS IS THE QUESTION THAT HAUNTED MY SOUL. SHE DID

23

NOT SEEM TO ACT ANY DIFFERENT. SHE WAS ALWAYS ANXIOUS TO SEE ME WHEN SHE ARRIVED OVER AT MY HOUSE OR WHEN I DROVE TO SEE HER. I WAS   SO NERVOUS. WOULD I SCARE HER OFF WITH THOSE THREE LITTLE WORDS? IF I WERE SAY IT WHEN WOULD I? AFTER MAKING LOVE OR BEFORE OR MAYBE AT DINNER OR MAYBE THE NEXT MORNING AS SHE FRANTICALLY SCAMPERED TO GET READY FOR WORK. SO I PLANNED FOR AFTER WE MADE LOVE THAT EVENING. AFTER A PASSIONATE EPISODE OF MAKING THE MOST PASSIONATE EPISODE OF EROTIC LOVE I HAD EVER KNOWN I QUIETLY WHISPERED INTO HER EAR ⱭI LOVE YOU@ . SHE LAY THERE SILENTLY NOT MAKING A SOUND. MY MIND WENT RACING. OH NO WHAT HAVE I DONE? DID I JUST MESS UP EVERYTHING? WHY! WHY! WHY! WHY DID NOT I WAIT A LITTLE LONGER, WHY DID NOT I SAY IT AT A DIFFERENT TIME, MAN I SCREWED UP, THESE THOUGHTS CIRCLED MY

24

HEAD A MILLION MILES PER HOUR. THEN I HEARD HER SLOWLY TAKE A BREATH IN AND THEN I HEARD IT. ⱥ I LOVE YOU TOOⱥ. YES! YES! YES! I COULD HARDLY CONTAIN MYSELF. I TURNED HER OVER GENTLY AND KISSED HER RED FULL LIPS. IT WAS INCREDIBLE. THE FEELING IN GORGED IN MY CHEST TO THE POINT I FELT IT WOULD EXPLODE. I WAS TRULY HAPPY. I FELT AS IF I OWNED THE WORLD AND FOR ONE MOMENT IN MY LIFE THE WORLD REVOLVED AROUND ME. THIS WAS MY MOMENT. I DID NOT NEED A CAMERA OR ANY OTHER RECORDING DEVICE. THIS MOMENT WAS BURNED INTO MIND LIKE A PHOTOGRAPHER'S NEGATIVES. THIS IS A DAY I WILL NEVER FORGET. THE NEXT DAY AT LUNCH I GOT A CALL AT WORK. IT WAS HER ON THE OTHER LINE. SHE SAID ⱥTHE FLOWERS WERE BEAUTIFULⱥ. I WAS GLAD, IT TOOK ME THIRTY MINUTES TO PICK THEM OUT. I DID NOT PICK ORDINARY ROSES, THE IDEA OF RED

ROSES SEEMED SO GENERIC TO ME. I PICKED ALL DIFFERENT COLORS OF ROSES WHICH WERE SURROUNDED BY ALL TYPES OF EXOTIC FLOWERS. SHE LOVED THEM. I WAS SO HAPPY. THINGS WENT ON GREAT FOR MONTHS TO COME. IT WAS SO GREAT. THE TIME RUSHED BY AS IF I WERE IN A TIME WARP. I RUSHED HOME RIGHT AFTER WORK JUST SO I COULD BE WITH HER. I HELD HER AND KISSED HER IN PUBLIC SO EVERYONE WOULD KNOW SHE WAS MINE. I WAS THE PROUDEST MAN ON EARTH AND NO ONE COULD TELL ME ANYTHING. IT WAS LIKE BEING FAMOUS WHEN I WALKED WITH HER DOWN THE STREET BECAUSE I FELT THAT ALL EYES WERE ON US. WE SHINED TOGETHER, BRIGHTER THAN ANY OTHER STAR IN THE SKY. THE COMBINATIONS OF OUR AURAS HAD THE MOST BRILLIANT COLORS INTER TWINED TOGETHER. AS THE MONTHS FLEW BY I SAVED AND SAVED LOOKING FOR YOU KNOW WHAT. I FINALLY FOUND WHAT I WAS LOOKING FOR AT

A FRIENDS JEWELRY STORE ON A LARGE PAGE DISPLAYED IN ONE OF THEIR CATALOGS. IT WAS A TWO PIECE RING WITH A HUGE DIAMOND THAT WAS CUT IN AN ODD WAY TOO ME. IT WAS NOT YOUR AVERAGE PRINCESS CUT, IT WAS A MARQUIS. IT WAS BEAUTIFUL AND SHINED WITH HER LIGHT. THAT WAS THE ONE. I FINALLY PAID OFF THE LAY AWAY AND THE RING CAME IN. IT WAS PRETTIER THAN THE PHOTO IN THE CATALOG. IT WAS GORGEOUS. I JUST HOPE SHE FEELS THE SAME. I WATCHED MANY MOVIES AND STUDIED ON THE WAYS TO OFFER A RING. THE CLASSIC DOWN ON ONE KNEE IN A CROWD, THE HIDE THE RING IN A PIECE OF FOOD STYLE, OR THE MAKE A NICE DINNER AND HIDE IT IN THE BREAD. I FINALLY MADE MY DECISION I WOULD PROPOSE AFTER DINNER LIKE A PRESENT STYLE ON OUR 1 YEAR ANNIVERSARY OF THE DAY WE MET WHICH WAS JUST WEEKS AWAY. AS I GOT HOME I JUST COULD NOT

WAIT. WHILE WE LYE IN BED THAT NIGHT I TOLD HER @I GOT SOMETHING FOR YOU TODAY ON THE WAY HOME@. I PULLED THE SMALL WRAPPED BOX FROM MY SOCK DRAWER AND HANDED IT TO HER. SHE SLOWLY UNWRAPPED IT AND SHE FELT SHE SUEDE BLACK BOX WITH THE TIPS OF HER FINGERS. I COULD HEAR THE TINY HINGES SNAP AS SHE OPENED THE BOX AND PEEKED INSIDE. I WATCHED AS HER EYES LIT UP AND GLOWED LIKE A STAR IN THE HEAVENS. AS SHE LOOKED AT ME SPEECHLESS I POPPED THE QUESTION. @WILL YOU BE MINE FOREVER AND A DAY?@ @WILL YOU MARRY ME?@ THE ROOM GOT SO QUIET I COULD HEAR THE WATER DRIPPING IN THE BATHROOM SINK. DRIP DRIP DRIP DRIP. HER SPEECHLESSNESS WAS KILLING ME. PLEASE SAY SOMETHING I SAID TO MY SELF. MY WHOLE LIFE HUNG IN THE BALANCE. ALL THE PLANS I HAD MADE IN MY HEAD AND US GROWING OLD TOGETHER. EVERYTHING WAS IN JEOPARDY AND IT HUNG

ON THOSE TWO WORDS. SHE LOOKED DEEP IN MY EYES AS IF SHE WAS TRYING TO READ MY MIND, AND THEN LOOKED DOWN AT THE RING. MY HEART WAS IN MY THROAT AND POUNDED LIKE A BASS DRUM IN A HIP HOP SONG. I THOUGHT IT WAS GOING TO COME OUT OF MY CHEST AND ONTO THE BED AND I WAS GOING TO DIE RIGHT THERE. SHE FINALLY LOOKED BACK UP WITH TEARS IN HER EYES. OF COURSE ILL MARRY YOU OF COURSE I WILL. I LOVE YOU WITH ALL MY HEART. WOOOOHOOOO. I HAD JUST BECOME THE RICHEST MAN IN THE WORLD. I HAD THE LOVE OF A WOMAN WHICH WAS WORTH TEN TIMES THE AMOUNT OF GOLD. IT WAS PRICELESS. I CANT BELIEVE IT GOD ONCE AGAIN COME THROUGH FOR ME. HE HAD HEARD MY PRAYER FROM EARLIER THAT NIGHT OR MAYBE HE ANSWERED HERS. I WAS THE PROUDEST MAN IN THE WORLD. AS WE WALKED DOWN THE STREET I WOULD TURN HER HAND SO EVERYONE COULD SEE THE

RING. EVERYMAN THAT PASSED BY NOW KNEW THAT SHE WAS MY SOON TO BE WIFE. IT WAS AMAZING. I FELT AS IF I WAS GOING TO EXPLODE. I HAD BEEN TRULY BLESSED. ME THE ONE WHO WAS NOT SO GOOD AT LOVE HAD DONE THE IMPOSSIBLE. I HAD LANDED THE GIRL OF MY DREAMS.

Chapter 4

The Haunting Past

THE NEXT YEAR WENT BY SO FAST, IT WAS INCREDIBLE. THE TIMES WE SPENT TOGETHER WERE UNBELIEVABLE. WE PURCHASED A HOME WITH A LOT OF LAND IN THE COUNTRY. WE FILLED IT WITH OUR THINGS NEW AND OLD. WE HAD MADE THIS PLACE A PART OF US AND I LOVED IT. OUR FAMILIES WERE HAPPY AND EVERYTHING WAS GOING GREAT. I WAS EXCELLING AT WORK AND SO WAS SHE. IT SEEMED THAT EVERYTHING WAS PERFECT BUT I WAS ABOUT TO DROP A BOMBSHELL THAT I HAD RECENTLY WORRIED ABOUT AS THE WEDDING DATE CAME CLOSER.

SHE HAD TOLD HER FAMILY AND EVERYTHING. HOW COULD I TELL HER THIS. I FELT SHE LOVED ME ENOUGH TO UNDERSTAND BUT I WAS STILL SO SCARED. I TOLD HER. I WAS AFRAID THAT MY DIVORCE FROM MY FIRST WIFE MAY NOT BE FINAL. I HAD NOT HAD CONTACT WITH MY EX IN QUITE SOME TIME. SHE WAS SO HURT I COULD SEE IT IN HER EYES. I PROMISED TO CALL THE LAWYER AS SOON AS POSSIBLE TO GET THIS MATTER RESOLVED QUICKLY. I WAITED PATIENTLY IN THE LAWYERS OFFICE THE NEXT MORNING EAGERLY TO TELL HIM MY STORY. I NEEDED THIS DONE AND DONE FAST. AS I ENTERED HIS OFFICE I COULD SEE PICTURES OF HIS WIFE AND KIDS ON THE TABLE. THEY LOOKED SO HAPPY AND I COULD NOT WAIT TO HAVE A PICTURE LIKE THAT OF MY FAMILY ON MY DESK. AFTER I EXPLAINED THE SITUATION TO HIM HE GAVE ME THE FEE. I WAS STUNNED, 750 DOLLARS. I SCRAPED UP THE MONEY OVER THE

NEXT FEW DAYS AND HURRIEDLY TOOK IT TO HIS SECRETARY. SHE RECEIPTED THE MONEY AND I LEFT WITH A GOOD FEELING. AS THE MONTHS SLOWLY ROLLED BY TOWARD OUR NEW WEDDING DATE I RECEIVED A PACKAGE IN THE MAIL. I LOOKED IT OVER AND IT WAS FROM THE LAW FIRM WHO WAS HANDLING MY DIVORCE. I HURRIEDLY OPENED IT HOPING TO FIND A COURT DATE INSIDE. AS I OPENED IT I SAW A CHECK INSIDE. ON A PIECE OF SOLID WHITE PAPER WHERE THE WORDS I DO NOT THINK I HAVE TIME TO DEAL WITH THE MATTER WE DISCUSSED AND IM REFUNDING YOUR MONEY. SORRY FOR ANY INCONVENIENCE THIS MAY CAUSE YOU. I WAS SO UPSET I HAD TO ASK HER TO CHANGE THE DATE ONCE AGAIN AND HAD TO START THE WHOLE PROCESS OVER. I HAD ALREADY LOST FOUR MONTHS WAITING ON THIS OTHER LAWYER. I BELIEVE SHE DID NOT BELIEVE ME. I THINK SHE THOUGHT I WAS STALLING

PURPOSELY TRYING NOT TO MARRY HER. THAT
WAS NOT THE CASE. I LOVED THIS WOMAN
WITH ALL MY HEART. THAT WAS THE TRUTH.
DAMN HOW COULD I HAVE BEEN SO STUPID.
WE STARTED ARGUING ALL THE TIME ABOUT
IT. I WISH I HAD NEVER MARRIED MY FIRST
WIFE. I MADE A MISTAKE, I WAS SO YOUNG
AND IT WAS JUST PLAINLY ONE OF THE
DUMBEST THINGS I HAVE EVER DONE. BUT WE
HAD LOVE AND I HAVE FAITH IN LOVE. I KNEW
IN THE BOTTOM OF MY HEART THAT LOVE
WOULD GIVE HER PATIENCE. WE HAD A BIG
BILL COME UP WHEN I GOT THE CHECK IN THE
MAIL SO I PAID IT WITH THE CHECK INSTEAD
OF REHIRING A NEW LAWYER AND BEFORE
YOU KNEW ANOTHER YEAR HAD PASSED. I
SCREWED UP BIG TIME. OVER THE LAST
COUPLE OF MONTHS. MONEY WAS TIGHT AND
IT SEEMED THAT SHE QUIT TALKING TO ME
AND STARTED CONFIDING IN HER FRIENDS.
WHEN WE WERE HOME TOGETHER IT WAS AS IF

I WE WERE HOME ALONE. SHED SCURRY TO THE BED ROOM AND JUMP ON THE PHONE AND I WOULD NOT TALK TO HER AGAIN TILL I WENT TO BED. I STARTED GOING OUT INSTEAD OF FIXING THE PROBLEM. SPENDING MY TIME IN THE BARS WITH MY FRIENDS WHO YOU GUESSED WERE SINGLE. I WAS LOSING HER AND I DID NOT EVEN SEE IT. AS THE MONTHS WENT BY WE GREW FURTHER AND FURTHER APART. SHE STARTED GOING OUT WITH HER FRIENDS AND ON SEVERAL OCCASIONS SHE NEVER CAME HOME. SHE WOULD HAVE SOME EXCUSE ABOUT PASSING OUT AT A FRIENDS OR SOMETHING LIKE THAT. I NEVER THOUGHT SHE WOULD DO WHAT SHE DID NEXT BUT I HAD IT COMING. I COULD NOT KEEP HER HANGING ON FOREVER. SOONER OR LATER IT WAS GOING TO HAPPEN AND TOMORROW MORNING IT WILL. EVERYTHING I BELIEVE IN FAILED ME AND I SAW THE LIGHT OF WHAT I HAD DONE WRONG. THE NEXT MORNING I SAW IT COMING UP THE

DRIVE IT WAS FOLLOWED BY SEVERAL CARS PACKED WITH PEOPLE. WHAT HAVE I DONE? WHAT HAVE I DONE? O' LORD WHAT HAVE I DONE? AS THE MOVING TRUCK SLOWLY CAME UP THE LONG DRIVEWAY AND BACKED UP TO THE STEPS. I WAS LATE FOR WORK SO I HURRIED OUT THE DOOR TO AVOID ANY CONFRONTATION. AS I WALKED TO MY TRUCK MY EYES MET THEIRS. IT WAS HER FAMILY AND THEY WERE NOT PLEASED. I DID NOT SAY A WORD I JUST CLIMBED IN MY TRUCK AND LEFT. WHEN I CAME HOME THAT NIGHT THE HOUSE WAS EMPTY EXCEPT FOR A FEW THINGS SHE HAD LEFT FOR ME. MY WORLD HAD BEEN TURNED UPSIDE DOWN. I WAS DEVASTATED. EVERYTHING WAS GONE. IT WAS A SHELL OF A HOUSE.

I WAS NOT PREPARED FOR WHAT HAPPENED NEXT. THIS WOULD TURN OUT TO BE THE LONGEST NIGHT OF MY LIFE. AS I LAID

THERE TRYING TO GOTO SLEEP THOUGHTS OF HER KEPT GOING THROUGH MY MIND. I MISSED EVERYTHING ABOUT HER. I MISSED HER TALKING ON THE PHONE. I MISSED HER SCRUBS LAYING ON THE FLOOR. I EVEN MISSED HER FUSSING AT ME, AND MOST OF ALL I MISSED HER WARM BODY AGAINST MINE. MY HEART FELT AS IF AN ELEPHANT HAD PUT HIS FOOT ON IT AND WAS PRESSING DOWN HARD AS HE COULD. LIKE EVERYTHING IN MY CHEST WAS JUST EMPTY. ALL NIGHT THOUGHTS OF HER RACED THROUGH MY HEAD. MY PHONE FINALLY WENT OFF AT TWO IN THE MORNING. I PICKED IT UP AND LOOKED AT THE CALLER ID. IT WAS HER .WHAT WAS SHE GOING TO SAY? WAS SHE MISSING ME OR DID SHE HATE ME? I ANSWERED THE PHONE AND IT WAS HER ON THE OTHER LINE. SHE SPOKE SO SOFTLY. ID BEEN LONGING TO HEAR HER VOICE SO BADLY I WOULD NOT EVEN CARE IF SHE CURSED ME FOR EVERYTHING I WAS WORTH. I WAS JUST

38

GLAD TO HEAR HER VOICE. SHE ASKED ME HOW WAS I DOING AND WAS I OK. I TOLD HER YES I WAS OK AND I WAS HAVING TROUBLE TRYING TO SLEEP BECAUSE I MISSED HER SO MUCH. SHE SAID SHE FELT THE SAME. I WAS RELIEVED THAT SHE WAS THINKING OF ME TOO. THAT MEANT THAT SHE STILL LOVED AND CARED ABOUT ME AND IT WAS MY MOVE TO MAKE THINGS RIGHT AND GET HER BACK. WE TALKED EVERY NIGHT FOR A COUPLE OF WEEKS, WE TALKED ABOUT SELLING THE HOUSE AND CLEARING UP SOME DEBT WE MADE TOGETHER. THAT IS WHEN IT HIT ME SHE WAS SNIPPING OFF ALL THE LOOSE ENDS THAT SHE NEEDED TO SNIP TO PREPARE FOR A LIFE ON HER OWN. MY HEART WAS BREAKING OVER AND OVER AGAIN. WHAT WILL I DO TO WIN HER LOVE BACK? I WAS SO STUPID. I MADE THE BIGGEST MISTAKE OF MY LIFE AND I HOPE I DO NOT SPEND THE REST OF MY LIFE PAYING FOR ITS CAUSE THERE WILL NEVER BE

ANOTHER HER AND I DO NOT THINK GOD SENDS MIRACLES TWICE. ALL I WANTED IN MY LIFE WAS HER AND SHE WAS SLIPPING THROUGH MY FINGERS. WHAT DO I DO? I HAVE NOT SLEPT OR ATE FOR DAYS AND THE THOUGHT OF HER BEING AWAY FROM ME WAS EATING ME UP INSIDE. I FELT LIKE I WAS DYING ON THE INSIDE. THE RING SHE ONCE WORE ON HER FINGER NOW FILLED AN EMPTY SPACE IN HER JEWELRY CHEST AND I WAS BECOMING A MEMORY IN HER SCRAPBOOK. WHAT DO I DO? HOW CAN I WIN HER BACK? I GUESS THAT IS UP TO ME. LET'S SEE WHAT HAPPENS.

Chapter 5

What will I Do?

WHAT CAN I DO, WHAT CAN I DO? THE QUESTION CIRCLED MY HEAD LIKE A TORNADO WITH BITS AND PIECES OF MISTAKES FLYING AROUND LIKE DEBRIS CAUGHT UP IN THE FURY OF THE HORRIFIC WINDS. THERE WERE NO ANSWERS. JUST BLAME, I JUMPED IN MY CAR AND ROAD OFF INTO THE NIGHT TO FILL A VACANCY ON A BARSTOOL AT A LOCAL BAR. THE ALCOHOL WENT DOWN SO SMOOTHLY TONIGHT. EVERY SONG THAT PLAYED ON THE JUKEBOX SEEMED TO CONJURE MEMORIES OF HER. THE ALCOHOLIC BLISS SEEMED TO TAKE THAT HEAVY FEELING IN MY HEART AND LIFTED IT IF ONLY FOR A LITTLE WHILE. AS I

DRANK THE MORE ENRAGED I BECAME AS IF I HAD AWAKEN SOME SLEEPING BEAST INSIDE OF ME. THEN LOGIC FELL VICTIM TO REASON WITH EACH COOL SWALLOW. I BEGAN TO BLAME HER. THIS IS HER FAULT, NOT MINE. SHE BETRAYED ME, SHE LEFT AND GAVE UP. I'M STILL HERE. IN THE BLISS I CALLED HER CURSING AND BLAMING HER FOR THE DOWNFALL OF OUR LOVE. THE ALCOHOL EITHER LOOSENED MY TONGUE OR IT BUILT A WALL. I DO NOT KNOW WHICH BUT I WAS DIGGING A WHOLE THAT WAS GOING TO BE IMPOSSIBLE TO GET OF. THE THINGS I SAID CAN NOT BE WRITTEN DOWN. WHAT A MISTAKE I MADE. SHE DID NOT CALL ME BACK THAT NIGHT BUT THE NEXT MORNING I GOT A CALL AND IT WAS NOT NICE. NEEDLESS TO SAY THIS WOULD BE THE LAST OF HER CALLS FOR SOME TIME TO COME. I STAYED IN THE HOUSE FOR A COUPLE OF DAYS BUT I COULD NOT STAND BEING THERE. EVERYTHING ABOUT THIS

HOUSE REMINDED ME OF HER. THE NEXT MORNING I PACKED MY BAGS AND THE FEW THINGS SHE LEFT BEHIND AND LOADED UP MY TRUCK AND LEFT THAT PLACE BEHIND. WHEN I PULLED OUT THE ;LONG DRIVEWAY I COULD SEE THE GHOST OF OUR LOVE STANDING ON THE PORCH WAVING AT ME LIKE AN ABANDONED CHILD WATCHING HIS PARENTS LEAVING NEVER TO RETURN. TEARS FILLED MY EYES AND THE PAIN I DRANK AWAY WAS BACK NOW TEN FOLD. I WENT TO MY FATHERS HOUSE AND MADE ME A COMFORTABLE PLACE TO SLEEP ON THE COUCH FOR A COUPLE OF DAYS TILL I COULD MOVE INTO A HOUSE I HAD JUST RENTED IN TOWN. IT WAS RIGHT IN THE MIDDLE OF WHERE I DID NOT WANT TO BE. I WAS A COUNTRY BOY WITH A TWENTY ACRE YARD NOW REDUCED TO LIVING IN A SMALL TINY HOUSE RIGHT IN THE SLUMS WITH NO YARD AND NO NATURE AT ALL EXCEPT MY SMALL GREEN YARD. THE WALLS HAD HOLES

THE CARPET WAS DIRTY, AND THE HOUSE REEKED OF SPOILED FOOD. I OPENED THE FRIDGE AND REALIZED WHY. BUT NOW AT LEAST I HAD SOMETHING TO SPEND MY TIME ON AND KEEP MY TIME OCCUPIED. I CLEANED THE CARPETS, SCRUBBED THE FLOORS, PATCHED HOLES IN THE WALLS, AND CLEANED THE FRIDGE. I MOVED MY STUFF IN IT AND BOUGHT WHAT I WAS MISSING. AFTER A WEEK OR TWO THE LITTLE HOUSE STARTED FEELING MORE LIKE A HOME. I LET A FRIEND MOVE IN THE SPARE BEDROOM AND WE WHERE ON THE PROWL. THERE WAS NOT A NIGHT THAT WENT BY WE DID NOT PARTY. THE SINGLE LIFE; OH HOW I HAD MISSED IT. MAYBE THIS IS WHAT I WANTED ALL ALONG. IT WAS LIKE MY LIFE WAS REPEATING ITSELF. FIND A GIRL FALL IN LOVE AND THEN LET HER RIP YOUR HEART OUT AND THEN START OVER. I WAS CAUGHT IN A PATTERN THAT I WAS DETERMINED NOT TO FOLLOW AGAIN. I WOULD NOT GET CLOSE TO

ANYONE. THE GIRLS CAME AND WENT AND MY HEART WAS SO HEAVILY GUARDED THEY NEVER HAD A CHANCE AT IT. THE WALL WAS THREE FEET THICK SOLID CONCRETE AND TOPPED WITH RAZOR WIRE. A WOMAN WOULD HAVE TO BE A MAGICIAN TO GET INTO THIS FORTRESS. FOR MONTHS THING WENT THE SAME TILL RING. GUESS WHO WAS ON THE LINE. IT WAS HER. HER VOICE SEEMED TO REMOVE THE DARKEN CLOUD THAT HAD BEEN HOVERING OVER ME. SHE ASKED ME HOW I WAS AND IF I WAS WELL. I TOLD HER YES I WAS FINE AND I LOVED MY NEW HOUSE. SHE ASKED IF SHE COULD DROP BY AND OF COURSE I SAID YES. THE FEELINGS I HAD BERRIED CAME RUSHING OUT OF THE GRAVE FASTER THAN I COULD THROW THE DIRT BACK ON TOP OF THEM. THE WALL I HAD BUILT HAD ONE FLAW. IT HAD A SMALL DOOR AND A LOCK WHICH ONLY SHE HAD THE KEY. I NEVER EVEN KNEW THE DOOR WAS THERE, BUT SURE ENOUGH IT

WAS THERE. DAMN HOW DUMB COULD I HAVE BEEN. HOW COULD I HAVE OVERLOOKED SUCH A BIG DEFECT IN MY DEFENSES? SHE CAME RIGHT BACK IN AND I COULD NOT DO A THING TO STOP HER. SHE HAD A UNSEEN POWER OVER MY HEART. IT WAS IF A PART OF IT WAS SLEEPING TILL SHE CAME ALONG AND THEN ALL AMOUNTS OF REASON WENT OUT THE WINDOW WITH THE SOFTNESS OF HER VOICE. I DOVE IN HEAD FIRST KNOWING IT WAS SHALLOW WATERS WILLING TO BEAR THE CONSEQUENCES OF MY ACTIONS. ALL CAUTIONS LIFTED AND I WAS IN LOVE ALL OVER. I STILL HAD ONE DEFENSE. MY MIND. MIND OVER MATTER. COULD IT WORK? MY HEART MAY FALL VICTIM BUT I NEVER WILL. I KEPT HER AT A DISTANCE AND STILL WENT OUT WITH MY FRIENDS. SHE MADE LATE NIGHT TRIPS AND IN THE DARKNESS OF MY ROOM SHE TOLD ME THINGS TO EASE MY DEFENSES AND TRIED TO MAKE HER WAY INTO MY LIFE AND

DESTROY WHAT I HAD CREATED. THE SINCE OF STABILITY WAS SLOWLY DETERIATING WITH EVERY PASSING DAY AS I FELL MORE AND MORE IN LOVE. WE MADE LOVE LONGER AND BETTER THAN EVER BEFORE AND THERE WAS NOT ANY RESTRAINT IN WHAT WE DID. IT WAS LIKE THE CHAINS WERE LIFTED THAT BONDED US TOGETHER WHICH WERE THERE WHEN WE LIVED IN THE SAME HOUSE. IT WAS INCREDIBLE BUT SOMETHING WAS WRONG. I TRIED TO SOLVE THE EQUATION SEVERAL TIMES BUT THE ANSWER WOULD NEVER CHECK OUT. SOMETHING WAS MISSING AND I DID NOT KNOW WHAT IT WAS.

Chapter 6

A Secret Is Revealed

SOMETHING IS WRONG IN ALL THIS BLISS. SOMETHING IS MISSING BUT WHAT WAS IT? SHE LOOKED THE SAME, SHE SMELLED THE SAME, AND SHE FELT THE SAME. WHAT COULD IT BE THAT WAS TROUBLING ME SO TERRIBLY DEEP INSIDE? I JUST CAN NOT FIGURE IT OUT. AFTER AWHILE SHE STOPPED COMING OVER LATER AT NIGHT BUT INSTEAD CAME OVER AFTER SHE GOT OFF WORK. SHE WOULD STAY ONE TO TWO HOURS AND THEN SHE WOULD SCURRY OUT THE DOOR TO HER FAMILY=S HOUSE WHO LIVED IN THE NEXT TOWN AN HOUR AWAY.I9 UNDERSTOOD. THESE ARE THE

SAME PEOPLE WHO CAME AND TOOK MY LIFE IN THAT MOVING TRUCK. THIS WENT ON FOR WEEKS, DAY AFTER DAY. I REMEMBER THE DAY CLEARLY SHE CAME OVER AT FOUR AND WE DECIDED TO RIDE TO TOWN TO PICK UP SOME FAST FOOD AND WE HEADED BACK HOME. I HAD AN OVERSIZED COAT ON THAT HAD BIG POCKETS AND DRABBED OVER ME AS IF IT WERE TWO SIZES TO BIG. I DID NOT CARE HOW IT LOOKED. IT WAS MY FAVORITE COAT AND I WORE IT EVERYWHERE. WE REACHED MY HOUSE AND SAT AT MY TABLE TALKING WHILE WE ATE OUR DINNER AND SHE STOOD UP AND SAID SHE MUST GO OR HER FAMILY WOULD GET WORRIED. I UNDERSTOOD, THEY WERE OLDER AND THEY DID WORRY ABOUT HER A LOT. I KISSED HER AT THE DOOR AND WALKED HER OUT AND TOLD HER TO CALL ME WHEN SHE GOT HOME TO LET ME KNOW SHE ARRIVED SAFELY. I WATCHED HER TAIL LIGHTS FADE AS SHE HURRIED DOWN THE DIRT

ROAD. ORANGE DUST ROSE FROM AROUND THE CAR AS SHE SPED DOWN THE DRY CLAY ROAD. IT HAD NOT RAINED FOR DAYS AND THE ROAD WAS SO DUSTY IT LOOKED AS IF A WINDSTORM BLEW THROUGH EVERY TIME A CAR WOULD PASS. EVERY TIME I WOULD COME HOME I WOULD HAVE TO RINSE THE RED DUST FROM MY CAR. AFTER ABOUT TEN MINUTES I NEEDED TO CALL MY DAD FOR SOMETHING AND NOTICED MY CELL PHONE WAS MISSING. I DID NOT HAVE A HOUSE PHONE BECAUSE TO ME IT WAS SENSELESS TO ME HAVING TO PAY TWO PHONE BILLS AND AS A SINGLE MAN I HAD TO SAVE WHERE I COULD. MY CELL PHONE HAD FALLEN OUT OF MY COAT AND INTO HER CAR SOMEWHERE. I RAN TO THE NEIGHBORS HOUSE AND CALLED MY NUMBER AND SHE ANSWERED. SHE SAID ªI HAVE YOUR PHONE AND SHE WAS HALF WAY HOME BUT SHE WOULD STILL TURNAROUND AND BRING IT@ THEN ALL OF A SUDDEN I HEARD A FAMILIAR

SOUND. A HIGH PITCHED BARK. I HEARD IT ECHO AS IF IT WERE BOUNCING OFF THE WALLS OF AN INCLOSED ROOM. IT WAS OUR DOG MOLLY. SHE WAS A BEAUTIFUL BLACK POMERANIAN WITH A WHITE STREAK THAT RAN DOWN HER CHEST. I COULD TELL THE BARK I HEARD WAS MY DOG CAUSE I MISSED THAT BARK THAT I HEARD SEVERAL TIMES BEFORE. SHE FINALLY ARRIVED BACK AT MY HOUSE TWENTY MINUTES LATER AND HANDED ME MY PHONE AND SAID ªI LOVE YOU@ AND THEN SHE SPED OFF DOWN THE ROAD. IT DID NOT SINK IN RIGHT AWAY. I GUESS IM NOT THE SHARPEST TOOL IN THE SHED SOMETIMES BUT THE PIECES STARTED TO FALL TOGETHER LATER THAT NIGHT AS I SAT ALONE AT MY FAVORITE WATERING HOLE. IT WAS A LITTLE JUKE JOINT I GUESS, NOT A WHOLE LOT OF PEOPLE , KIND OF RUNDOWN, AND A JUKEBOX THAT SILL PLAYED RECORDS THAT WERE GROSSLY OUT DATED. ITS WAS A PLACE

WHERE YOU DRANK YOUR BEER FROM THE BOTTLE AND ON HOT DAYS YOU OPENED THE DOOR TO LET THE BREEZE THROUGH. THIS WAS MY KIND OF PLACE. I LOVED IT HERE. I HAD MADE A LOT OF FRIENDS WITH THE REGULARS. AS I DRANK SEVERAL BEERS MY MIND RACED AROUND IN CIRCLES ADDING MINUTES AND TAKING AWAY SECONDS. HOW COULD I HAVE HEARD THAT DOG IF SHE LEFT MY HOUSE TWENTY MINUTES AGO AND IT TAKES HER AN HOUR TO GET HOME? I FELT AS IF I WAS SHERLOCK HOMES. THIS WOULD HAVE TO TAKE SOME CANNING INVESTIGATIVE WORK. I DID NOT WANT TO ALARM HER SO I DID NOT CALL. I DEVISED A PLAN. I HAD HEARD RUMORS OF HER LIVING SOME WHERE ELSE BUT SHE ASSURED ME THIS WAS NOT THE CASE. SHE PROMISED ME AND SHE HAD NEVER BEEN CAUGHT IN A LIE BEFORE SO I TRUSTED HER. I GRABBED THE PHONE BOOK OFF THE BAR AND THUMBED THROUGH THE SECTION

THAT WOULD CONTAIN HER LAST NAME, BUT HER NAME WAS NO LISTED ANYWHERE. I PLACED THE BEER STAINED, TORN, AND TATTERED PHONE BOOK BACK AT THE END OF THE BAR AND HEADED OUT THE DOOR. I HAD ONE VALUABLE ASSET AT HOME I HAD NOT TRIED YET, THE INTERNET. I TYPED HER NAME IN THE SPACE PROVIDED AND BAM, THERE IT WAS ALL OVER MY COMPUTER. AN ADDRESS POPPED UP AND IT WAS ONLY MINUTES FROM MY HOUSE AND SHE HAD A LOCAL TELEPHONE NUMBER. I DECIDED NOT TO CALL HER AND WAITED FOR THE CLOCK TO STRIKE MIDNIGHT BEFORE I WOULD MAKE MY MOVE WHEN I KNEW SHE WOULD BE SOUND ASLEEP. WHEN THE CLOCK STRUCK MID NIGHT I JUMPED IN MY TRUCK AND RODE OFF FOLLOWING THE DIRECTIONS I HAD DOWNLOADED OFF MY COMPUTER. AS I MADE MY WAY I NOTICED THE STREETS WERE EMPTY, NOT EVEN A COP RIDING AROUND. I FOLLOWED THE DIRECTIONS

TO A T. I FOLLOWED THE HIGHWAY TO TOWN, THEN GOT ON MAIN STREET, FOLLOWED IT TILL I TURNED LEFT BY A RESTAURANT AND THEN TO THE STOP SIGN. FINALLY I WAS ON HEARD RODE. I NERVOUSLY READ THE NUMBERS ON EACH HOUSE COUNTING DOWN TOWARDS HER HOUSE. DAMN! I MUST HAVE MISSED IT. I TURNED AROUND AND WENT BACK DOWN THE STREET LOOKING CLOSER. THERE WAS ONE HOUSE ON THE STREET WITH NO LIGHTS ON THAT I COULD NOT SEE THE NUMBER ON AND GUESS WHAT? THAT@S RIGHT, IT WAS HER=S. I NOW SEE WHY I DID NOT SEE HER CAR FOR IT WAS PARKED IN THE BACK IN A DARK ALLEY WAY.

Chapter 7

The Call

AS I APPROACHED HER HOUSE AN
UNFAMILIAR CAR WAS IN HER DRIVE AND I
COULD SEE REFLECTIONS FROM HER TAIL
LIGHTS IN FRONT OF HIS CAR PARKED BETWEEN
A ROW OF HEDGES THAT LINED HER DRIVEWAY.
THAT IS WHY I DID NOT SEE HER CAR. IT WAS
THERE ALL ALONG JUST WELL HIDDEN IN THE
DARK. BUT WHO IS CAR COULD THIS BE HAD
SHE GOTTEN A ROOMMATE. OR MAYBE IT WAS
HIM. THE MYSTERIOUS JODY I HEARD SO MUCH
ABOUT IN THE MILITARY. THE MAN YOUR WIFE
LEFT THE DOOR UNLOCKED FOR WHILE YOU
WHERE ON DEPLOYMENT. WHO COULD IT BE. I
CALLED HER CELL OVER AND OVER AND IT

WENT STRAIGHT TO VOICE MAIL, I KNEW SHE HAD IT OFF SO I CALLED 411. I GAVE THE OPERATOR THE INFORMATION AND SHE CAME BACK WITH A NUMBER. I WROTE THE NUMBER DOWN ON MY WORK PAD AND THEN SHE TRANSFERRED MY CALL. THE PHONE RANG AND RANG THEN FINALLY SHE ANSWERED HALF AWAKE. SHE WAS STARTLED WHEN SHE REALIZED WHO WAS ON THE PHONE AND THEN I HEARD HIM SAY BABE WHO IS IT. I WAS DEVASTATED ALL OVER AGAIN BUT THIS TIME MUCH, MUCH WORSE. MY HEART FELL TO THE FLOOR AND I BEGAN TO CURSE VIOLENTLY INTO THE PHONE AND THEN I HUNG UP AND SPED BACK TO MY WATERING HOLE TO DRINK MY SORROWS AWAY ONCE MORE. I WAS FURIOUS. I HAD BEEN BETRAYED TWICE BY THE WOMAN I LOVED BUT I WAS NOT GOING TO GIVE UP. THIS MAN HAD TOOK MY PLACE AND NOW I KNOW I HAD BECOME THE JODY I HAD MUCH FEARED. I WAS HIS JODY. HE PROBABLY

WAS A NICE GUY AND HAD NO IDEA OF ME EITHER. I CALLED HER HOME NUMBER ON MY CELL FROM THE BAR AND WAITED. IT WAS AFTER TWO AND SHE NEVER PICKED UP BUT THE ANSWERING MACHINE DID. I DEVISED A PLAN THAT WOULD PAY HER BACK FOR HER SELFISHNESS. I SPOKE LOUD AND CLEAR INTO THE PHONE SO THE ANSWERING MACHINE WOULD BROADCAST MY MESSAGE LOUD AND CLEAR AS THEY LAY THERE IN THE DARK. I TOLD HER HOW BETRAYED I FELT AND THAT I APPRECIATED HER DAILY VISITS TO MY HOUSE AND HOW I HAD ENJOYED OUR SEXUAL INTERLUDES FOR THE LAST MONTH. I KNEW THEY COULD HEAR ME. HE DESERVED TO KNOW THE TRUTH AND I LAID IT OUT THERE. I LEFT NO STONE UNCOVERED I TOLD IT ALL IN DETAIL TILL I HEARD HER PICK UP AND SLAM THE PHONE DOWN. HER SCAM WAS THROUGH. SHE WAS BUSTED. AND ALL THAT WAS LEFT WAS MY SHATTERED HEART. THE NEXT DAY I HEARD

RUMORS FROM MY FRIENDS WHO HAD SEEMED TO ALREADY HAVE KNOWN BUT KEPT IT HIDDEN FROM ME. I WAS FURIOUS. HOW COULD THEY KEEP THIS FROM ME? MAYBE THEY WERE TRYING TO PROTECT ME. OR MAYBE THEY DID DROP HINTS AND I JUST WAS NOT WILLING TO ACCEPT THEM. HOW DUMB COULD I HAVE BEEN? THE SIGNS WERE THERE. SHE WAS ON A TIME LINE THAT IS WHY HER VISITS WERE CUT SHORT. I ALSO FELT SORRY FOR HIM BECAUSE I KNEW HE WAS GOING THROUGH THE SAME THING BUT LATER I LEARNED THEY WERE SEEING EACH OTHER BEFORE SHE LEFT ME SO I HAD NO PITY. I WAS GETTING TO THE BOTTOM OF THIS MYSTERY ONLY TO FIND THERE WAS NOT ONE. THE BARREL WAS BOTTOMLESS IT JUST SEEM TO GO ON AND ON. BUT I HAD NOTHING BUT TIME ON MY HANDS AND MY HANDS WERE ALREADY DIRTY WITH THE BUCKET FILLED FILTH. I DO NOT GIVE UP EASY I HOPE THIS GUY KNOWS HE IS IN FOR A FIGHT. I

WILL NOT LIE DOWN AND DIE. TOMORROW I WILL START A NEW LEAD AND LEAVE THIS CRAP BEHIND. HE CAN HAVE HER AND HER DECEIVING WAYS. IF SHE DECEIVED ME SHELL DECEIVE HIM. THAT IS MY PHILOSOPHY. I BELIEVE IN LOVE I JUST DO NOT HAVE FAITH IN IT MUCH ANYMORE AND I KNOW THE SAYING DO NOT LET A FEW BAD APPLES SPOIL THE BUNCH BUT IM BEGINNING TO THINK I GOT A BAD BUNCH OF APPLES AND IM TRYING TO FIND ONE GOOD APPLE THAT SLIPPED IN BY ACCIDENT. IS MY HEART CURSED? I KNOW IM NOT THE BEST MAN OUT THERE BUT IM CERTAINLY NOT THE WORST BY FAR. I HAVE MY FAULTS AND TO ME THERE NOT VERY MAJOR BUT TO SOMEONE ELSE I GUESS THEY ARE. WELL I HEAR THE LAP BAR CLICKING AS IT COMES DOWN OVER ME. THE OPERATOR CHECKS IT TO SEE IF ITS SECURE. THEN I FEEL THE JOLT OF THIS ROLLER COASTER TAKING OFF AGAIN. IM GETTING USED TO THE UPS AND

DOWNS IT'S JUST THOSE LOOPS THAT GET ME
EVERY TIME. THIS IS A RIDE I FEEL I'M READY
TO GET OFF. IT MAY BE A DIFFERENT COASTER
BUT THE RIDE ALWAYS ENDS THE SAME.

Chapter 8

Out of the Starting Gate

I WILL FIGHT FOR HER. NO MAN WILL
TAKE WHAT IS MINE. MY MIND RACED FASTER
AND FASTER. I DINT SLEEP AT ALL THAT
NIGHT. I JUST LAY THERE MAKING FACES AND
IMAGES OF THE STUCCO PAINTED CEILING. I
FELT NAUSEOUS AND ACHING ALL OVER. THE
THOUGHTS SPUN SO FAST AROUND MY HEAD I
COULD NOT CONCENTRATE ON JUST ONE.
FINALLY THE MOMENT HAD FINALLY COME IN
CAME A BRIGHT ORANGE BAND ACROSS THE
ROOM WORKING ITS WAY SLOWLY UP MY
WALLS SUCH AS A GIANT PAINT BRUSH. I
COULD FEEL THE WARMTH ENTERING THE

ROOM. I HAD MADE IT. I MADE IT THROUGH THIS DARK NIGHT AND IM ALIVE AND STRONGER NOW.

I HURRIED OFF TO WORK AND AS I SIT THERE I WATCHED THE PHONE. ALMOST WISHING IT TO RING. I WANTED SOME KIND OF RESPONSE TO THE BRAVE AND DARING ACT I HAD SO STRATEGICALLY CARRIED OUT THE NIGHT BEFORE. IT NEVER RANG. THE DAY WENT BY SLOWLY AS THE NEXT TILL ALMOST A WEEK HAD GONE BY. FINALLY IT RANG AND IT WAS HER. SHE SPOKE SOFTLY AND ALMOST FORGIVING TONE. SHE KNEW SHE HAD BEEN WRONGDOING AND THAT SHE WAS CAUGHT. THERE WAS NO DENYING IT. SHE CAME OUT WITH THE TRUTH AND TOLD ME ALL ABOUT HIM AND HOW HE LEFT STORMING OUT THAT NIGHT BUT THAT HE WAS STILL CALLING HER. HE WANTED TO RECONCILE BUT SHE DID NOT KNOW WHO SHE LOVED. I TOLD HER I CANT

LIVE THIS WAY. I FEEL LIKE A PIECE OF MY HEART DIES EVERY DAY AND SOON THERE BE NOTHING LEFT BUT AN EMPTY HOLE. SHE ASKED ME TO COME OVER TO HER HOUSE THAT NIGHT AND EAT DINNER WITH HER. I SHOWED UP AT EXACTLY 7PM. WE SAT AT THE DINNER TABLE AND QUIETLY ATE. THEN MADE OUR WAY TO THE COUCH WHERE ON THE TABLE WAS A KEY. SHE SAID THAT IS YOURS AND I WANT YOU TO STAY WITH ME. THIS IS SO UNEXPECTED. SHE CHOSE ME OVER HIM. MAYBE HE DID NOT HAVE THE HOLD ON HER HE THOUGHT HE HAD. THE FIRST WEEK I TRIED TO DO EVERYTHING I COULD THINK OF TO CORRECT THINGS I HAD NEGLECTED IN THE PAST. I KISSED HER A LITTLE MORE. I COOKED DINNER. I CLEANED UP MY CLOTHES OFF THE FLOOR. I TOOK OUT THE TRASH. I DONE EVERYTHING I COULD DO TO LET HER KNOW I WAS BACK AND I MEANT TO MAKE THIS FICKLE THING CALLED LOVE TO LAST. EVERYDAY WAS

BETTER AND BETTER. SHE TOLD ME SHE LOVED ME MORE AND MORE EACH DAY AND EACH DAY I FELT SHE MEANT IT MORE AND MORE. WEEK TWO WAS EVEN BETTER. WE DONE THINGS TOGETHER INSTEAD OF APART. WE WATCHED TV TOGETHER, WENT OUT TO DINNER, WENT TO THE MOVIES, AND CUDDLED TOGETHER FOR HOURS AT THE TIME. FRIDAY I GOT OFF WORK AND WALKED IN THE DOOR. SHE WAS SITTING THERE ON THE COUCH WITH A SADDENED LOOK ON HER FACE. I ASKED HER WHAT WAS WRONG BUT SOME HOW I KNEW. HER EYES WELLED UP WITH TEARS AND SHE BEGAN TO SLOWLY SPEAK. I SAT DOWN AND I STARED INTO HER BLUE EYES AND THE WORDS CAME LIKE STONES HITTING ME AT 90 MPH IN THE FACE. MY PRIDE, EGO AND MANHOOD WAS BEING DESTROYED. MY FAITH IN LOVE CRUSHED TO SMITHEREENS BEFORE MY EYES. SHE TOLD ME SHE WAS STILL IN LOVE WITH HIM AND THAT SHE WOULD LIKE HER KEY

BACK. I SLOWLY TOOK IT OFF MY KEY CHAIN AND LAID IT ON THE COFFEE TABLE. I TRIED TO THINK OF THE WORDS TO SAY BUT I COULD NOT. THEY JUST WOULD NOT COME OUT. IT WAS AS IF AN INVISIBLE GAG HAD BEEN PLACED OVER MY MOUTH. I SLOWLY OPENED THE DOOR AND WALKED OUT. SHE JUST SAT THERE STARING AT THE FLOOR.

I RODE ALL THE WAY HOME THINKING TO MYSELF. WHAT WAS WRONG WITH ME, I THOUGHT THE GOOD GUYS WON. I GUESS THAT IS ONLY IN THE MOVIES. IN THIS MOVIE THE GOOD GUY LOSES. OR MAYBE THE OTHER GUY IS BETTER THAN ME. HAVE I BECOME THE BAD GUY? THE MAN IN THE BLACK COWBOY HAT WHO ALWAYS GETS IT IN THE END. LOOKING AT MY TRACK RECORD IT MIGHT JUST BE. AS I SAT BACK AT MY FAVORITE HOLE IN THE WALL I ORDERED UP ONE MORE BEER FOR THE NIGHT. MY FRIEND SAT THERE BESIDE ME LIKE

HE HAD DONE MANY NIGHTS BEFORE ASKING WHERE I HAD BEEN FOR THE PAST TWO WEEKS. I TOLD HIM AND ASKED IF HE WOULD GIVE ME A RIDE SOMEWHERE. AS WE ROAD TOWARDS HER HOUSE HE GAVE ME ADVICE ON LOVE BUT I TOOK IT WITH A GRAIN OF SALT BECAUSE HE WAS AT THE BAR EVERY NIGHT TOO. WHAT DID HE KNOW THAT I DID NOT? HE JUST GOT OFF THE RIDE DID NOT GET BACK IN LINE AGAIN. WHY SHOULD I TAKE ADVICE FROM A QUITTER? WE NEARED HER HOUSE AND I GOT ANSWER TO A QUESTION I HAD BEEN ASKING MYSELF ALL DAY. YES THERE WAS HIS CAR. SHE GAVE HIM MY KEY AND SO EASILY HE FILLED MY PLACE. I HOPE SHE CHANGED THE SHEETS (LOL). WE MADE OUR WAY BACK TO THE BAR AND I UNDERSTOOD WHAT MY FRIEND WAS TALKING ABOUT. WHY PUT MYSELF IN A POSITION WHERE I CAN GET HURT. MAYBE I SHOULD JUST LOVE THEM AND LEAVE THEM. WHEN I GO OUT JUST SIMPLY

LEAVE MY HEART AT HOME AND DO NOT INVOLVE THE WORD SEX WITH LOVE. THEY ARE NOT THE SAME. LOCK MY HEART AWAY IN A LITTLE BOX AT HOME IN THE CLOSET AND LEAVE IT THERE AND ENOJOY THE SINGLE LIFE. RIDE THE ROLLER COASTER I DESIGNED. THIS MIGHT BE THE BEST RIDE OF THEM ALL.

Chapter 9
My Own design

THE NEXT GIRL I MEET WILL RIDE ON MY COASTER. SHE CAN GET OFF WHEN SHE LIKES AND SHE CAN GET ON AS LONG AS I LET HER. I CAN CHOOSE WHEN TO CLOSE THE RIDE OR TO LET SOME ONE RIDE AGAIN WITHOUT WAITING IN LINE. YES THIS MY ANSWER. THIS IS WHAT I'LL DO. HOW HARD CAN THIS BE I HAVE SEEN ALL MY FRIENDS DO IT FOR YEARS. THAT NIGHT I MATICOUSLY GOT READY. I SHOWERED, BRUSHED MY TEETH, PUT ON MY DEODERANT AND WALKED INTO MY CLOSET. I SHUFFLED THROUGH HANGERS OF SHIRTS AND PANTS TO FIND THE BEST ONE. I GRABBED MY

NICEST SHOES AND WHITEST PAIR OF SOCKS. I WORE MY SILK BOXERS. I WAS DRESSED TO THE T. I SLOWLY COMBED MY HAIR GETTING EVERY STRAND IN THE RIGHT PLACE. I SPLASHED ON SOME EXPENSIVE COLOGNE, GRABBED MY CELL, AND OUT THE DOOR I WENT. I STOPPED BY THE CAR WASH AND WASHED MY TRUCK AND VACUUMED OUT THE INSIDE. I EVEN BOUGHT ONE OF THOSE LITTLE TREES THAT SMELL LIKE THE BEACH. IF A WOMAN GOT IN MY TRUCK TONIGHT SHE WOULD SEE A MAN WHO REALLY HAS HIS SHIT TOGETHER. EXCUSE THE FRENCH. TONIGHT MY SEAT AT THE LOCAL BAR WILL BE VACANT FOR ANOTHER LONELY SOUL FOR I WONT BE THERE. I WENT TO A NEW BAR TONIGHT AND THEY HAD KARIOKE AND I FEEL I SING PRETTY GOOD. IM NOT THE BEST THERE IS BUT IM STILL BETTER THAN MOST I GUESS. I DO NOT WANT TO TOOT MY OWN HORN YOU KNOW. I SCROLLED THROUGH THE BOOK NOT TALKING

TO NOONE. I PICKED OUT SOME VERY POPULAR SONGS WITH THE LADIES AND WAITED MY TURN. FINALLY MY NAME WAS CALLED AND I WALKED ON THE STAGE. THE FIRST SONG I SANG WAS A COUNTRY SONG THAT I KNEW THE GOOD OLE BOYS IN THE BAR WOULD LIKE. THIS WOULD MAYBE MAKE THEM LIKE ME AND NOT GIVE ME ANY TROUBLE. AFTER I WAS DONE THE WHOLE PLACE WAS STANDING AND CLAPPING. THE OLE BOYS WERE PATTING ME ON THE BACK AS I WALKED BACK TO MY SEAT. I WATCHED THE WOMEN WHISPERING TO EACH OTHER AS THEY WATCHED ME SIT DOWN. I KNEW EXACTLY WHAT THEY WERE WHISPERING WHO IS THIS GUY. SEE I ALWAYS WORE A HAT SO I WAS HARD TO RECOGNIZE. I ONCE HAD SOMEONE COME UP AND THEY THOUGHT I WAS BALD BECAUSE I ALWAYS WORE THE HAT. I HAVE VERY THICK BLACK HAIR. I'M NOT BALD OR BALDING. IN MY FAMILY ALL THE MALES HAVE HAIR TILL THEY

74

DIE THEY JUST HAVE ONE DRAW BACK. THEY ALL USUALLY HAVE SALT AND PEPPER HAIR BYE THE AGE OF 35. IM 29 NOW SO I GUESS I GOT A COUPLE GOOD YEARS LEFT. I PICKED OUT ANOTHER SONG THIS TIME SHOWING AN EMOTIONAL SIDE. IT WAS ONE OF THOSE TEAR JERKING COUNTRY SONGS. I SUNG IT TRYING NOT TO MAKE EYE CONTACT WITH ANYONE THERE. AS I FINISHED ONCE AGAIN THE AUDIENCE STOOD UP AND CLAPPED BUT THIS TIME THE LADIES STOOD UP TOO. THEY WHERE SHOUTING AND CLAPPING AND YES STILL WHISPERING. SONG AFTER SONG I SANG EACH ONE AS GOOD OR BETTER THAN THE FIRST. AND AS MYSTERIOUSLY AS I ARRIVED I LEFT WITHOUT TALKING TO A SOUL, NOT EVEN THE BARTENDER. TWO NIGHTS LATER I FOUND MYSELF BACK THERE ON THE NEXT KARIOKE NIGHT AND IT WAS IF EVERYONE KNEW MY NAME. AS I WALKED TO A VACANT BAR STOOL THE MEN REACHED OUT THERE HAND AND

SHOOK MINE AND CALLED ME BY MY NAME.
THE LADIES GAVE ME A HUG AND ASKED HOW
I WAS. IT WAS IF I HAD BEEN COMING HERE FOR
YEARS. BEER AFTER BEER ROLLED IN FROM
THE LADIES. THE HARD PART NOW WAS NOT TO
GET TO DRUNK AND MAKE AN ASS OUT OF MY
SELF. EVERY SLOW SONG THAT PLAYED THERE
WOULD BE A LADY ASKING ME TO DANCE. IT
WAS CRAZY. NOONE HAD EVER ASKED ME TO
DANCE BEFORE BUT SURE ENOUGH THEY
WERE. I DANCED ALL NIGHT AND WITHOUT
SAYING A WORD TO ANY OF THEM SLIPPED
OUT AGAIN. I WENT BACK AGAIN AND AGAIN
AND BEFORE LONG EVERYONE KNEW MY
NAME AND WHO I WAS. I EVEN WENT OUT ON A
COUPLE OF DATES. IT WAS GREAT. I HAD
BECOME THE MAN I ALWAYS WANTED TO BE. I
WAS MYSTERIOUS AND THE LADIES LIKED ME.
ONE BY ONE THEY TRIED TO GET TO KNOW ME
ANY WAY THEY COULD. I WOULD HAVE A
SHORT RELATIONSHIP WITH THEM LETTING

THEM KNOW UP FRONT I DID NOT WANT TO BE TIED DOWN AND THAT I WAS SEEING OTHER PEOPLE. THEY DID NOT CARE. STILL THEY CAME THEY SHARED MY BED AND TRIED TO GET TO MY HEART. AS SOON AS I FELT THEM GETTING CLOSE OUT THE DOOR THEY WENT. I NEVER LEFT ON A BAD NOTE THOUGH EXCEPT ONCE AND THAT IS ANOTHER STORY (LOL). THE WOMEN ACCEPTED IT AND TREATED ME AS IF I WERE THERE TROPHY. IT WAS GREAT BUT SOMETHING WAS MISSING. WHAT WAS IT. I WAS HAPPY FOR AWHILE BUT IT STARTED GETTING OLD. I HAD MADE SO MANY NEW FRIENDS BUT I WAS STILL LACKING ONE THING AND IT WAS IN MY CLOSET LOCKED UP IN A STRONG BOX. IT WAS MY HEART. SHOULD I GET IT DOWN AND LET ONE OF THESE LADIES IN OR SHOULD I JUST KEEP GOING THE WAY I HAVE BEEN. EVERYTHING WAS GOING GREAT FOR ME SO WHY SHOULD I CHANGE IT.

Chapter 10
Something I Found

I CHOSE TO LEAVE MY DAMAGED HEART IN ITS BOX TO HEAL WHILE I KEPT MAKING MY WAY TO THE CLUBS. NIGHT AFTER NIGHT TILL ONE NIGHT I GOT SOMETHING I HAD NEVER GOTTEN BEFORE. BY THIS TIME I KNEW THE BARTENDERS BY NAME AND WE WERE FRIENDS. SARAH SLOWLY PLACED A BEER ON THE THIN CARDBOARD ADVERTISEMENT COASTER IN FRONT OF ME AND WHISPERED THIS IS FROM A SECRET ADMIRER. WOW, I HAD NEVER HAD ONE OF THESE BEFORE. I BEGGED HER TO TELL ME WHO SENT IT BUT SHE NEVER WOULD. TRUE TO THE PROMISE SHE HAD MADE

TO THE SENDER. BEER AFTER BEER CAME NIGHT AFTER NIGHT. I SLOWLY SCANNED THE ROOM WATCHING THE EYES OF THE LADIES AROUND THE ROOM. SO MANY OF THEM WERE LOOKING AT ME. WHO COULD IT BE? I HAVE NO EARTHLY IDEA. I WISH SHE WOULD LEAVE ME ONE CLUE BUT SHE NEVER DID. I DEVISED A PLAN TO FIND WHO THIS MYSTERY LADY IS. I ORDERED A DRINK THAT WAS VERY COLORFUL AND BRIGHT. ONE THAT NO OTHER LADY IN THE ROOM WAS DRINKING. I KNEW WHEN THE BARTENDER DELIVERED ALL I HAD TO DO IS SEE WHO WAS DRINKING IT AND I WOULD KNOW. SARAH CAME BACK AND SAID SHE DID NOT ACCEPT THE DRINK BUT SHE WOULD CHANGE IT TO WHAT SHE WAS DRINKING AND THANK S FOR THE ROUND. DAMN SHE WAS SMART. SHE OUTWITTED ME TIME AFTER TIME. SARAH ALWAYS TOOK FOUR OR FIVE DRINKS AT THE TIME TO DIFFERENT LADIES TO HELP CAMOUFLAGE HER TRAIL. SHE WAS THERE IN

THE CROWD. A HEART LONGING FOR ME BUT WHO WAS SHE. I HAVE NEVER IN MY 29 YEARS BEEN SO STUMPED. NIGHT AFTER NIGHT WENT BYE. THE BARTENDERS AT THIS PLACE ARE VERY LOYAL THEY NEVER WOULD TELL. JAMES AND MICHELLE AND JULIA. THEY ALL STUCK BY THERE STORY. I CANT TELL YOU WHO SENT THE DRINK AND THEY ALL COVERED THERE TRACKS. THIS WAS SO CRAZY. SO FINALLY I STARTED MEMORIZING EACH LADY THAT WAS IN THE BAR AT A SPECIFIC NIGHT. SO IF THERE WAS A NIGHT THE DRINK DID NOT COME I MAYBE WOULD HAVE A BETTER IDEA OF WHO HAD SENT IT. NIGHT AFTER NIGHT THE DRINKS CAME BUT NOONE WAS THERE EVERY TIME THE DRINK CAME. THIS WAS ONE FOXY LADY. SHE WAS SO CLEVER. SHE COULD SMELL THE AMBUSHES BEFORE I EVEN LAID THE TRAPS. THIS GAME WAS ALMOST ANNOYING BUT ALSO SO FUN. IT WAS LIKE A BITTER SOUR CANDY. THE BITTER

WENT SO WELL WITH THE SOUR IT MADE YOU WANT IT MORE AND MORE. ONCE AGAIN THOUGHTS RACED THROUGH MY HEAD. I WOULD IMAGINE MYSELF LYING IN BED WITH HER WITH CANDLES BURNING AROUND THE ROOM, WAIT HAVE I JUST BECAME A ROMANTIC MAN. WHERE DID THAT COME FROM? THIS LADY WAS CHANGING ME AND I DID NOT EVEN KNOW IT. I WAS FALLING FOR HER AND I DID NOT EVEN KNOW WHO SHE WAS. I WOULD IMAGINE HER SMELL, HER FEEL, AND THE TASTE OF HER LIPS. HER SOFT BODY LAYING AGAINST MINE IT WAS CRAZY. HOW COULD THIS BE? I RUSHED HOME AND OPENED THE BOX IN MY CLOSET AND IT WAS STILL THERE. MY HEART LAY THERE IN THE BOX, GREY AND DECAYING IT WAS DEAD. SO WHERE WERE THESE FEELINGS COMING FROM? THEN I REALIZED WHEN I REMOVED MY HEART MY BODY SIMPLY GREW A NEW ONE. NO MATTER HOW MANY TIMES I WOULD REMOVE IT AND

LOCK IT AWAY EVENTUALLY A NEW ONE WOULD GROW IN ITS PLACE. I REALIZED I CANT HIDE FROM LOVE. I CAN HIDE FOR A WHILE BUT SOONER OR LATER IT WILL FIND ME. I WAS HIDING WELL BUT NOW THE RULES HAD BEEN REVERSED. I WANTED HER SO BADLY. AT NIGHT THOUGHT OF HER FILLED MY SLEEP. I DREAMED OF HER SO OFTEN BUT I COULD NEVER SEE HER FACE. IT WAS LIKE TORTURE THAT FELT GOOD. WEIRD HUH? I STARTED BECOMING SCARED THAT I MAY BUILD MYSELF UP FOR A BIG LET DOWN. WHAT IF SHE WAS NOT WHAT I HAD DREAMED? WHAT IF SHE WAS NOT MY TYPE AT ALL? I GUESS I JUST HAVE TO HAVE FAITH IN LOVE. WHAT IS THAT I HAVE FAITH NOW? ALL THESES THINGS ARE COMING BACK I THOUGHT I HAD TOSSED AWAY FOR GOOD. PLEASE LET HER BE THE ONE I DO NOT KNOW HOW LONG I CAN GO ON LIKE THIS. WHO IS SHE? WHO IS THIS MASKED LADY? WHO IS THIS GHOST WHO HAUNTS MY

THOUGHTS AND DREAMS? I MISS THIS WOMAN SO MUCH BUT I DO NOT EVEN KNOW HER. IT IS THE MOST INSANE THING I KNOW BUT IM CAUGHT UP IN IT. I HOPE THIS IS WORTH IT. I REALLY DO. MAYBE SHE WILL REVEAL HER SELF TONIGHT. WELL JUST HAVE TO WAIT AND SEE. THIS IS THE LAST NIGHT BEFORE CHRISTMAS EVE AND I HAVE TO GO OUT OF TOWN FOR A FEW DAYS. PLEASE LET IT BE TONIGHT. WHAT A GREAT CHRISTMAS PRESENT THIS COULD BE. I HURRIED TOWARD THE BAR BREAKING THE SPEED LIMIT AND CHANCING EVERY YELLOW LIGHT. I MADE IT. 9 O=CLOCK ON THE DOT. I WALKED IN AS USUAL BUT STILL SEARCHING TRYING TO READ THE FACES OF THE LADIES AROUND ME. HELLO, HELLO HOW ARE YOU, IM FINE . ALL THE WAY DOWN THE STARES I GREETED AND SHOOK HANDS AS I MADE MY WAY TO MY FAVORITE STOOL AND I SAT DOWN AND THERE IT WAS RIGHT IN FRONT OF ME. A BROWN BOTTLE FILLED TO THE TOP

BREWED BARLEY AND HOPS. THE SWEAT DRIPPED OFF THE COLD BOTTLE. I GRABBED MY MONEY TO PAY FOR IT AND THE BARTENDER LAUGHED AND SAID IT IS TAKEN CARE OF. DAMN ALREADY, I JUST GOT HERE. THIS IS SO UNREAL. I DRANK THE FIRST SECOND THIRD TILL FINALLY IT WAS TIME TO GO. I GUESS TONIGHT IS NOT TONIGHT. MAYBE ILL NEVER FIND OUT. MAYBE SHE IS MARRIED OR HAS A BOYFRIEND OR MAYBE SHE IS JUST THAT SHY. I STILL HAVE NO CLUES AND ITS TIME TO GO. I WALED OUT THE DOOR AND GOT INTO MY TRUCK AND MADE MY WAY HOME. AGAIN AND AGAIN THOUGHTS CIRCLED MY MIND. IT WAS SO CRAZY. WHO WAS THIS WOMAN? I GUESS I MAY NEVER KNOW. WAS SHE THE ONE I WAS LOOKING FOR OR WAS SHE TO BECOME ANOTHER CHAPTER IN MY LIFE THAT SOME HOW MADE ME STRONGER. WAS I THE ONE SHE HAD BEEN WAITING FOR OR WOULD SHE BECOME ANOTHER CHAPTER IN

MY LIFE OF MESS UPS? I WISH GOD COULD
SOME HOW GIVE ME A SIGN SO I COULD AVOID
ALL THE CONFUSION AND HEARTACHE. MAYBE
TOMORROW NIGHT ILL KNOW WHO SHE IS OR
MAYBE GOD WILL LET HER FADE OUT OF MY
LIFE AS MYSTERIOUSLY AS SHE APPEARED.
WHAT WAS TO BECOME OF ME, ONLY HEAVEN
KNOWS? ONLY HEAVEN KNOWS. THE SECRET I
WANTED SO BADLY TO BE REVEALED WHICH
WAS STILL HIDDEN AMONGST THE SHADOWS
CAST BY THE NEON LIGHTS WHICH DANCED ON
THE WALLS OF THE OLD SMOKEY BAR. WHO
WAS SHE? WHO WAS SHE? I HAD EXHAUSTED
ALL MY RESOURCES. I HAD NO MORE
INGENIOUS PLANS AND EVEN IF WE MET AND
ALL WAS GRAND WHY WOULD I THINK FOR
ONCE THAT IF WE MET WHY WOULD THIS BE
ANY DIFFERENT THAN THE RELATIONSHIPS
BEFORE. THE NEXT I SCURRED BACK TO THE
BAR WHEN ONCE AGAIN THER WAS A BEER IN
MY SPACE. I AST THERE DRINKING THE FREE

BEER MORE FRUSTRATED THAN EVER. HOW I WANTED TO MEET THE LADY. I WAS OUT OF IDEAS AND READY TO GIVE UP WHEN. SARAH, THE OFF DUTY BARTENDER, WALKED OVER WITH ANOTHER BEER. SHE PLACED IT IN FRONT OF ME AND ASKED'HAVE YOU FIGURED IT OUT YET?" "NO" I SAID IN FRUSTRATION STARING AT THE HEAVY GRAINED BAR. SHE LOOKED AT ME AND WHISPERED IN MY EAR"IT'S ME, I SENT THE DRINKS. I'VE BEEN SEEING SOMEONE BUT ITS OVER NOW BETWEEN US. THAT'S WHY I COULDN'T TELL YOU", SHE WHISPERED. SHE TOLD ME SHE HAD WANTED TO TELL ME FOR A WHILE BUT COULDN'T. HER AND THE MAN SHE HAD BEEN SEEING WHERE FINALLY THROUGH. A SLOW SONG CAME ON AND SHE GRABBED MY HAND AND LED ME TO THE DANCE FLOOR. OH MY GOD, I HAD LIKED HER FOR SO LONG. SARAH WHO HAD TURNED ME DOWN COUNTLESS TIMES BEFORE WAS MY SECRET

ADMIRER AND I WAS NOW GONNA DANCE WITH HER.

Chapter 11
A Beautiful Thing

AS THE DANCE WAS COMING TO AN END I SAW SARAH=S EYES GET LARGE AND A WORRIED LOOK QUICKLY CAME OVER HER FACE. WHAT IS WRONG AND THEN THEIR WAS A TAP ON MY SHOULDER. I LOOKED BACK AND THEIR HE WAS. IT WAS THE MAN THAT HAD BEEN WITH HER ALL THOSE TIMES BEFORE. THEY WENT TO THE EDGE OF THE DANCE FLOOR WHERE THEY STARTED ARGUING. I HEARD HER TELL HIM TIME AND TIME AGAIN THAT SHE DID NOT LOVE HIM ANYMORE. HE WAS NOT GIVING UP THAT EASY AND HE PLEADED WITH HER OVER AND OVER AND SHE

90

JUST TURNED AWAY. WHAT HAD THIS MAN DONE TO LOSE A LOVE WITH THIS LADY? I FELT BAD SO BAD FOR HIM. I HAD BEEN THEIR BEFORE AND I KNEW HOW IT FELT TO HOLD ONTO A WOMAN WHO WAS LETTING GO. HE TURNED AWAY FROM HER AND SCURRIED OUT THE DOOR. THEIR WAS ANGER AND PAIN ALL OVER HIS FACE. AS SHE WALKED BACK TO ME SHE JUMPED AS THE DOOR SLAMMED SHUT BEHIND HIM. SHE APOLOGIZED AND SAID SHE HAD TO LEAVE. WE EXCHANGED NUMBERS AND OUT THE DOOR SHE WENT. THE BARTENDER WORKING THAT NIGHT GLANCED OVER AND SMILED. I GUESS YOU CAN TELL NOW I CAN KEEP A SECRET SHE SAID AS SHE WAS WIPING DOWN THE LACQUERED BAR TOP. YES YOU CAN I HAD NO IDEA. I PAID MY TAB OUT AND HEADED BACK HOME. MAN I CANT BELIEVE ITS HER THE MAN I HAVE LIKED FOR YEARS. I TRIED TALKING TO HER BEFORE AND SHE ACTUALLY GOT RUDE WITH ME BEFORE.

NEXT THING YOU KNOW IM LAYING IN MY BED AND THOUGHTS OF HER RACED THROUGH MY HEAD. I COULD NOT GET HER OUT. I LAID THEIR ALL NIGHT STARING AT THE CLOCK IMAGINING ME AND HER TOGETHER TWENTY YEARS FROM NOW. I IMAGINED HOW HER BODY WOULD FEEL LYING NEXT TO MINE. IT WAS AN AWESOME FEELING. THE NIGHT WENT BY SO SLOWLY. I COULD NOT WAIT TO GET UP TOMORROW AND CALL HER. FINALLY THE SUN CREPT UP AND OUT OF BED I JUMPED. I GOT DRESSED FOR WORK AND THEN NOTICED IT WAS TWO HOURS BEFORE I EVEN HAD TO BE THEIR. I MADE MY WAY TO THE LOCAL BREAKFAST RESTAURANT AND SAT AT MY USUAL SEAT. I ORDERED MY BREAKFAST AND HAD A CUP OF COFFEE. I WAS SO EXCITED ABOUT MY DAY AHEAD. FINALLY I GOT TO THE JOB SITE AND STARTED WORKING. FINALLY 12 O=CLOCK CAME AND I DIALED HER NUMBER. WHEN SHE ANSWERED HER VOICE FILLED MY HEART. I LOVED THE WAY SHE

SOUNDED. HER VOICE WAS UNIQUE AND WAS SO SWEET. IT WAS LIKE ONE I HAD NEVER HEARD BEFORE. SHE TOLD ME SHE HAD BEEN WAITING FOR ME TO CALL ALSO AND THAT SHE FELT THE SAME WAY LAST NIGHT. SHE TOLD ME SHE COULD NOT WAIT TO HAVE ME I HER ARMS AGAIN SO WE MADE PLANS TO MEET UP THAT NIGHT AT THE BAR. AFTER HURRYING HOME AFTER WORK I QUICKLY GOT DRESSED AND RACED TO THE BAR. SHE WAS THEIR AT THE DART BOARDS WHEN I WALKED IN AND SHE LEAPT OVER TO ME. WRAPPING HER ARMS AND LEGS AROUND ME LIKE I WAS HER BROTHER WHO JUST CAME HOME AFTER SERVING A TOUR IN THE GULF. SHE KISSED ME HARD AND PASSIONATELY. OUR LIPS FIT TOGETHER PERFECTLY LIKE THEY WERE MEANT FOR EACH OTHER. WE ST DOWN AT THE BAR AND HAD A COUPLE OF DRINKS AND WE HEADED OUT THE DOOR TOA LOCAL DANCE CLUB. THE NIGHT WAS PERFECT, WE HAD SO

MUCH FUN. TOWARDS THE END OF THE NIGHT THE DJ PLAYED A SLOW SONG SO WE MADE OUR WAY TO THE DANCE FLOOR FOR OUR LAST DANCE OF THE EVENING. SHE THREW HER ARMS AROUND ME AND PRESSED HER BODY NEXT TO MINE. I SLOWLY BENT DOWN AND KISSED HER NECK AND TASTED HER SWEET SKIN. HER PERFUME LINGERED IN THE AIR AND IT SMELLED LIKE FIELDS OF JASMINE. I HELD HER SO CLOSE TO ME TRYING TO BREATHE HER COMPLETELY IN. I SLID MY HAND UNDER THE BACK OF HER SHIRT PLACING MY HAND DIRECTLY ON THE FLESH ON THE SMALL OF HER BACK. HER SKIN WAS SO SOFT AND SUBTLE LIKE A ROSE PEDAL. HER EYES TWINKLED IN THE LIGHT OF THE ROTATING STROBES. I LOOKED UP AND ONCE AGAIN IT WAS HIM. HE HAD FOLLOWED US HERE. HE GRABBED HER ARM JERKING HER TO THE SIDE. OH NO NOT THIS TIME. I GRABBED HER OTHER ARM AND PULLED HER BACK TO MY SIDE. HE

STARED INTO MY EYES. I WATCHED THE TWITCHING OF HIS HANDS. I WATCHED FOR ANY SIGN THAT HE WOULD SWING ON ME, BUT HE NEVER DID. HE JUST WALKED AWAY AND OUT THE DOOR HE WENT. AFTER WE FINISHED OUR DANCE WE SAID GOODBYE TO OUR FRIENDS AND HEADED OUT THE DOOR. WE DROVE TO MY HOUSE TALKING AND JOKING AND HAVING A BLAST. WE PULLED IN THE DRIVE AND WALKED IN THE HOUSE. WE BOTH KNEW WHY WE WHERE HERE BUT WE WERE BOTH TO SCARED TO SAY IT. AS SHE WALKED IN I SPUN HER AROUND AND PULLED HER CLOSE TO ME AND PRESSED MY LIPS TO HERS. I CARESSED HER BODY GENTLY BUT FIRMLY. SHE LIFTED MY SHIRT AND PULLED IT OVER MY HEAD AND TOSSED IT ON THE FLOOR. HER HANDS LAY ON MY BARE CHEST AND SHE NAVIGATED HER HANDS AGAINST MY BARE SKIN AS TO SEE WITH HER HANDS LIKE THE BLIND DO. I TOOK OFF HER SHIRT AND TOSSED

IT ON TOP OF MINE AND OUR BARE FLESH RUBBED TOGETHER. WE DISROBED AND MADE OUR WAY TO THE QUEEN SIZE BED WHERE I EMBRACED HER ON THE THICK COMFORTER. I KISSED EVERY INCH OF HER BODY BREATHING IN EVERY BIT OF HER. WE MADE PASSIONATE LOVE OVER AND OVER. I WATCHED AS THE EXPRESSIONS ON HER FACE CHANGED AS I DROVE HER CLOSER TO EXTACY. THE LOVE WE MADE WAS LONG AND SWEET. I COULD NOT GET ENOUGH OF HER. THIS WAS SOMETHING BEAUTIFUL IN THE MAKING.

Chapter 12

Falling Again

THE NEXT DAY AT WORK I RECEIVED A CALL AT AROUND NOON AND IT WAS HER. ID BEEN WAITING FOR HER CALL. HER VOICE WAS SOFT AND SWEET AND SHE ASKED IF I COULD COME OVER TO HER PLACE FOR LUNCH. I TOLD HER YES AND GOT IN MY TRUCK AND DOWN THE ROAD I WENT. I READ THE DIRECTIONS TURN HERE GO THERE AND 3RD HOUSE ON THE RIGHT. THERE WAS HER CAR. I PULLED IN THE DRIVE AND WALKED TO THE DOOR. I KNOCKED ON THE GLASS SCREEN DOOR AND I HEARD HER YELL TO COME ON IN. AS I WALKED IN THERE WAS A HALL TO MY LEFT AND I HEARD

95

HER VOICE AGAIN SAY IM BACK HERE. I MADE THREE STEPS IN THAT DIRECTION AND BEFORE THE FOURTH SHE RAN AT ME LEAPING INTO MY ARMS. SHE HELD ME OH SO TIGHTLY AND PULLED ME TOWARDS A ROOM AT THE END OF THE HALL. WE WALKED IN AND IT WAS HER BEDROOM. SHE WALKED BACKWARDS PULLING ME TO THE BED AND SHE LAID DOWN NEVER LETTING GO OF MY HANDS SO I WOULD BE PULLED DOWN ON TOP OF HER. WE KISSED AND WELL YOU KNOW WHAT HAPPENS NEXT. DAY AFTER DAY WE WERE TOGETHER. WE COULD NOT SEEM TO GET ENOUGH OF EACH OTHER. IN A WEEKS TIME SHE TOLD ME SHE LOVED ME AND I TOLD HER THE SAME. I TRULY DID LOVE HER. SHE WAS INSTILLED IN MY HEART AND SOUL. I COULD BARELY EVEN CONCENTRATE AT WORK FOR THINKING ABOUT HER. WEEK AFTER WEEK WENT BYE AND THE LOVE GREW STRONGER AND STRONGER. I WOULD GOTO WORK WITH HER AT

NIGHT AND SIT TILL CLOSING TIME JUST TO HAVE A CHANCE TO BE NEAR HER. WE WENT EVERYWHERE TOGETHER. ALL OF OUR FRIENDS APPROVED OF US BEING TOGETHER AND COMMENTED DAILY HOW GOOD WE WERE TOGETHER. IT SEEMED SHE HAD A ROUGH LIFE BEFORE ME WITH MEN. I WOULD TREAT HER WAY BETTER THAN ANYONE HAD EVER TREATED HER BEFORE THAT WAS MY GOAL. NOTHING ELSE WOULD EVER MATTER. SLOWLY I FOUND MYSELF DISTANCING MYSELF FROM FRIENDS AND FAMILY FOR HER. I MADE HER MY WORLD. THE OTHER WOMEN AROUND US TOOK NOTICE OF HOW WELL I TREATED HER AND MADE COMMENTS TO ME ON HOW THEY WOULD HAVE LIKED TO HAVE MET ME BEFORE HER BUT IT WAS TOO LATE FOR THEM FOR MY HEART BELONGED TO HER. SHE WAS MY EVERYTHING AND MY WORLD REVOLVED AROUND HER. USUALLY LOVE FOR ME HAD GROWN WEAKER OVERTIME BUT THIS WAS

DIFFERENT, SHE WAS MY ONE. THE ONE YOU WAITED FOR ALL YOUR LIFE. I HAD FINALLY FOUND THE LOVE THAT YOU ONLY SEEN IN THE MOVIES. WHEN WE LAY TOGETHER I CARESSED THE SMOOTHNESS OF HER SKIN TOUCHING EVERY IMPERFECTION ON HER BODY NOTICING HOW THEY ADDED UP TO PERFECTION. WHAT AN IRONIC TWIST. HER SKIN WAS AS SMOOTH AS WHEN YOU TOUCH A ROSE OR DAISY PEDAL. IT GLIDED UNDER MY ROUGH CALLUSED FINGERS. HER SMELL WAS OF A FIELD OF JASMINE IN FULL BLOOM. WHEN I TOUCHED HER MY PASSION ROSE SO HIGH I FELT AS IF I WAS IN ANOTHER WORLD. EVERYTHING REVOLVED AROUND US AND HER WHISPERS IN MY EAR WAS OF THE SWEETEST SYMPHONIES. I COULD NOT KEEP MY MIND ON MY WORK. I WOULD TRY TO CONCENTRATE BUT I COULD NOT. I WOULD START ON SOME OVERDUE PAPERWORK AND THEN I WOULD WAKE FROM A DAYDREAM OF HER AND ME

AND FIND THAT ALMOST AN HOUR HAD GONE BY. HOW CAN THERE BE SUCH A LOVE AND IT WAS MINE. I WOULD FIND MY SELF IN DAYDREAMS OF LAYING WITH HER STARING INTO HER DEEP BLUE EYES AND ALMOST TASTING HER SWEETNESS. YES YOU GUESSED IT SOME OF THE DAYDREAMS WERE EROTIC BUT NEVER X RATED. THEY WERE PURELY ROMANTIC. I COULD NOT SEE HER IN ANY OTHER WAY. HOW COULD A HEART THAT HAD BEEN TORN TO HELL AND BACK COME BACK SO STRONG. OH YES I WAS IN TROUBLE. I WAS IN LOVE LIKE NO OTHER I HAD EVER KNOWN. LORD PLEASE HELP ME BECAUSE I KNOW NOT WHAT I HAVE DONE. I COULD NOT EVEN LOOK AT ANOTHER WOMAN. IT WAS ALL HER, EVERY EMOTION, EVERY THOUGHT, EVERYTHING I HAD CONSISTED OF HER. OH YES IM IN TROUBLE DEEP.

Chapter 13

Passion Rises High

DAYS AND DAYS WENT BY AND THINGS ONLY GOT BETTER. WE WERE SO SPONTANEOUS IT WAS INSANE. NEVER HAVING A PLAN WE JUST DONE WHAT WE FELT. WE CAME TOGETHER NIGHT AFTER NIGHT AND I NEVER GOT TIRED OF IT. EVERY NIGHT WAS LIKE A NEW ADVENTURE. WE NEVER MADE LOVE THE SAME WAY TWICE. WE TOOK LONG SHOWERS TOGETHER TILL THE HOT WATER RAN OUT. THE LOVE I HAD FOR HER HAD TURNED INTO AN OBSESSION. I WAS LIKE A JUNKIE ON A STREET CORNER WILLING TO ROB AND SELL EVERYTHING I COULD GERT MY HANDS ON FOR

JUST ONE MORE FIX. IT WAS CRAZY. AFTER ABOUT FOUR MONTHS I NOTICING A CHANGE IN HER AND IT LITERALLY SCARED THE HELL OUT OF ME. IT WAS LITTLE CHANGES THAT WERE VERY SUBTLE. SHE STOPPED MEETING ME AT THE DOOR WHEN I GOT HOME. AT NIGHT WHEN I HELPED HER CLOSE THE BAR I STARTED NOTICING HER EX COMING BACK AROUND. I LET MY HEART BLIND ME FROM ALL THE SIGNS. THE ROMANTIC NIGHTS WERE GETTING FEWER AND FEWER AND WHEN I ASKED WHAT WAS WRONG SHE WOULD GET AGGRAVATED MORE AND MORE. THE MORE SHE DENIED ME THE MORE I NEEDED HER. I WAS DRIVING HER CRAZY. HOW CAN YOU LOVE SOMEONE TO MUCH? THIS GAME IM PLAYING MAKES NO SENSE TO ME. THE RULES KEEP CHANGING AND SOME HOW I WAS NOT INFORMED. I CAN SEE WHERE THIS WAS HEADING AND I TRIED AND TRIED TO STOP THE WHEELS OF FATE FROM TURNING BUT NOTHING I DID WOULD HELP. SHE MADE

EXCUSES WHY WE WERE NOT BEING INTIMATE
BUT I DID NOT BUY THEM. I KNEW WHAT WAS
GOING ON AND I COULD NOT DO A DAMN THING
ABOUT IT. DOWN THE HILL I GO AND YOU
GUESSED IT I HAVE NO BRAKES AND IM
DODGING TREES LEFT AND RIGHT GETTING
FASTER AND FASTER ON EACH LONG STRAIGHT
AWAY. I WAS IN UNCHARTED TERRAIN AND
AROUND EACH BEND THERE WAS ANOTHER
GROVE OF PINES. IT WAS A FRIDAY NIGHT AND
WE WENT OUT TO THE BAR WHERE SHE
WORKED FOR A FEW DRINKS. A LOT OF HER
FRIENDS WERE THERE SO WE THREW SOME
DARTS WITH THEM AND JUST HUNG OUT. I SAW
SOME FRIENDS DOWN AT THE BAR SO I WALKED
OVER TO THEM AND STARTED TALKING AND I
LOOKED UP AND THERE HE WAS. HE WAS UP
THERE TALKING TO THE LOVE OF MY LIFE. LIKE
A THIEF IN THE NIGHT HE WAS PRYING AT HER
DEFENSES TO FIND A WEAKNESS SO HE COULD
STEAL BACK HER HEART. I GAVE HER A LOOK

AND WENT BACK TO MY CONVERSATION. SOON AFTER SHE CAME TO ME AND ASKED ME TOO STEP OUTSIDE ONTO THE COVERED PORCH TO TALK. AS I THE DOOR SLAMMED BEHIND US I COULD HEAR IT IN HER VOICE. MY HEART FELL TO MY STOMACH CAUSE I KNEW IT WAS COMING. THE ONE PINE TREE THAT I COULD NOT SWERVE TO MISS AND BAMM I HIT IT HARD. SHE TOLD ME I WAS A GREAT GUY BUT SHE JUST DID NOT LOVE ME ANYMORE. I FOUGHT BACK THE TEARS AS HARD AS I COULD. SHE PULLED ME CLOSE TO HE BUSSOM AND HUGGED ME AND KISSED ME DEEPLY AND TURNED AND WALKED AWAY. I COULD NOT SAY A WORD. THE LUMP IN MY THROAT SUFFOCATED MY VOCAL CORDS AND EVERY SOUND I TRIED TO MAKE FELL SHORT. I TOOK ONE MORE LOOK IN HER EYES AND TURNED AND WALKED AWAY. OH NO TO NIGHT IS GOING TO KILL ME. I WENT TO ANOTHER BAR DOWN THE ROAD WHERE SOME OF MY FRIENDS WERE. THOUGHTS OF HIM

AND HER RACED THROUGH MY MIND AS I INHALED BEER AFTER BEER. THERE WAS A TAP ON MY SHOULDER AND I SLOWLY TURNED AROUND. IT WAS GLORIA FROM THE BAR I JUST LEFT. SHE TOLD ME HOW SHE THOUGHT OF ME ALL THE TIME AND WAS JUST WAITING ON THE OPPURTUNITY TO BE WITH ME. SHE WATCHED THE BREAK UP AND FIGURED NOWS HER CHANCE. LIKE AND LION AFTER ITS PREY SHE HAD WATCHED FROM THE HIGH GRASS WAITING FOR ME TO BE VULNERABLE AND NOW WAS THE TIME. WE SAT THERE AND TALKED AND TALKED. THE MORE I STAYED THE DRUNKER I GOT. AS I STOOD UP TO PAY FOR MY NEXT BEER SHE REACHED HER HAND DEEP IN MY POCKETS AND TOOK MY KEYS. SHE TOLD ME THAT I WAS IN NO CONDITION TO DRIVE AND THAT SHE WAS TAKING ME HOME TONIGHT. BEER AFTER BEER WENT BY TILL I DIDNT EVEN REMEMBER WHY I WAS THERE. NEXT THING I REMEMBER I WAS IN THE

PASSENGER SIDE OF MY TRUCK WITH MY HEAD OUT OF THE WINDOW WITH THE WIND RUSHING THROUGH MY HAIR. WE WEREN'T GOING TOWARDS MY HOUSE THOUGH. I DIDN'T KNOW THESE STREETS AT ALL. LEFT AND THEN RIGHT. WE WERE IN THE DOWNTOWN AREA AND FINALLY WE STOPPED AT A SMALL COTTAGE TYPE HOUSE. AS SHE REMOVED THE KEYS SHE LOOK AT ME AND THROUGH THE GLOW OF THE DASH LIGHTS SHE ASKED ME WAS I COMING IN OR WAS I GOING TO STAY IN THE TRUCK ALL NIGHT. I SLOWLY OPENED THE DOOR AND FOLLOWED HER IN TO THE LIVING ROOM. SHE THEN TURNED AND PULL ME CLOSE TO HER BODY ALMOST RIPPING MY SHIRT OFF. SHE WAS VERY AGGRESSIVE. I WATCHED AS MY SHIRT HIT THE FLOOR AND THEN SHE UNBUCKLED MY BELT AND PULLED THROUGH THE RUNGS IN MY JEANS IN A FAST MOTION AND FLUNG IT ACROSS THE ROOM. BEFORE I KNEW IT I WAS IN MY BOXERS AND SHE WAS PULLING ME

106

TOWARDS HER BEDROOM. I WANTED TO RESIST BUT THOUGHTS OF SARAH AND HER EX RACED THREW MY HEAD. HELL IF SHE COULD DO IT SO COULD I AND IN I WENT. SHE WAS SO AGGRESSIVE BUT I KIND OF LIKED IT AND AS WE HAD SEX AND YES SEX WAS ALL IT WAS I THOUGHT ABOUT SARAH. I FOUND MY SELF BEING AGGRESSIVE. THE LOVING SIDE OF ME WAS GONE AND WE JUST GOT NASTY. IT WAS PASSIONATE BUT NOT IN A ROMANTIC WAY. EVERY THRUST AND PUSH WAS NOT TO BRING HER EXTACY BUT TO JUST MAKE HER MOAN LOUDER. LOUDER AND LOUDER SHE BECAME UNTIL WE WERE FINISHED. LITTLE DID I KNOW THIS DROVE HER WILD AND I WOULD HAVE TROUBLE FROM THEN ON? WHAT HAVE I DONE? THIS IS NOT ME. I HAVE BECOME A MONSTER. I LET SOMEONE MANIPULATE ME AND CHANGE ME INTO SOMETHING IM NOT OR MAYBE THIS WAS WHO I WAS ALL ALONG. MY FAMILY HAD A HISTORY OF USING WOMEN. MY BROTHER AND

MY DAD WERE SINGLE AND BOUNCED FROM GIRL TO GIRL. I GUESS I JUST LEARNED WHAT THEY KNEW ALL ALONG. DO NOT LOVE JUST HAVE SEX? LEAVE YOUR EMOTIONS AND FEELING S AT HOME PUT UP ON A SHELF. I SHOULD HAVE LEARNED THIS LESSON BEFORE BUT I GUESS I WAS THE SLOW ONE FOR I NOTICED A TREND I HAD SAT. THE NICER AND MORE LOVING I WAS TO WOMEN THE MORE I GOT HURT AND NOW THAT I THINK OF IT ALL THE GUYS WHO TREATED THERE LADIES SHITTY WERE STILL TOGETHER. OH NO THEY HAVE CREATED A MONSTER AND IT IS A LIVE AS LIGHTNING CRASHES AND THE LARGE GURNY IS LOWERED FROM THE OPENING IN THE CEILING WITH ME ON IT. YES NOW MORE THAN EVER I HAD LOST FAITH. EVERYTHING I BELIEVED IN WENT RIGHT OUT THE WINDOW AND I WAS A CHANGED MAN. WHY DID LOVE CHOOSE ME? WELL IT WILL NEVER HAPPEN AGAIN. THIS HEART IS STONE AND A MONSTER CANT LOVE.

Chapter 14

The Monster Is Loose

I STAYED AWAY FROM WHERE SARAH WORKED AND FOUND NEW BARS TO FREQUENT. AS THE SUN STARTED TO SET I COULD FIND THAT I WOULD TRANSFORM. I HAD BECOME EVERYTHING I HATED. I BOUNCED FROM BAR TO BAR. NIGHT AFTER NIGHT I SHARED MY BED WITH ANOTHER LADY. I HAD SOME GREAT LINES. I WOULD PROMISE THE WORLD BUT THEY WERE ALL EMPTY. THERE WAS NO TRUTH TO ANY OF IT. I USED THE ILLUSION CREATED BY ME TREATING SARAH GOOD TO MY ADVANTAGE. BEFORE I KNEW IT I WAS JUGGLING 4 OR 5 RELATIONSHIPS WITH DIFFERENT WOMEN AND NOONE KNEW NOTHING. I TREATED EACH ONE AS IF THEY WERE THE LOVE OF MY LIFE

AND THEY FELL FOR IT HOOK, LINE AND SINKER. I WATCHED AS THEY FELL DEEPER AND DEEPER IN LOVE WITH ME. OH YES I WAS A MONSTER. WHEN ONE STARTED ACTING CRAZY OR TOO LOVING I WOULD JUST SIMPLY STOP CALLING HER. IT WAS LIKE SHE NEVER EXISTED AND I WOULD WATCH AS THEY CALLED OVER AND OVER AGAIN. I WOULD JUST LET THE PHONE RING AND RING AND AFTER A WEEK OR TWO THEYD QUIT CALLING. I STARTED PERFECTING MY BODY BY WORKING OUT AND GETTING A TAN SO I COULD CATCH MORE AND MORE PREY. WHEN I WALKED INTO A BAR I WOULDNT SAY ANYTHING TO ANYONE I WOULD JUST SIT THERE AND NO MATTER WHERE I WAS I COULD CATCH LADIES CHECKING ME OUT. I WOULD STARE DEEP INTO THERE EYES FROM ACROSS THE ROOM AND THEN LOOK DOWN AND BEFORE YOU KNEW IT SHED BE SITTING BESIDE ME AND THEN HERE IT WOIULD COME. I LAID IT ON THICKER THAN MOLLASSES. THE GIRLS WOULD EAT IT UP NO MATTER WHAT AGE. I WAS THIRTY AND THEY WOULD RANGE FROM 18 TO 35. THE MONSTER INSIDE HADNT DEVOURED ALL OF ME

THOUGH BECAUSE I FELT THEIR PAIN AND FELT SORRY FOR THEM. THE WAY I SAW IT THOUGH WAS I GOT MINE WHO CARES ABOUT THEM BUT I DID. I JUST TOSSED ANY FEELING I WOULD GET OUT THE WINDOW AND KEPT TREDGING UP THAT HILL. THIS LIFE STYLE SEEMED TO SUIT ME GOOD. AFTER AWHILE I STARTED GOING OUT OF TOWN ON WEEKEND AND FOUND MYSELF WITH TWO OR THREE WOMEN OUT OF DIFFERENT TOWNS ALSO. I COULDNT EVEN MANAGE IT ALL. MY CELL PHONE STEADILY BLEW UP. IT WOULD GET SO BAD THAT I HAD TO TURN IT OFF SOME TIMES WHEN I WAS WITH OTHER WOMEN. I STARTED FINDING MYSELF BACK AT THE BAR WHERE SARAH WORKED BUT I STUFFED THE FEELINGS DOWN SO DEEP IT DID NOT EVEN BOTHER ME TO SEE HER THERE WITH HIM. I STILL LOVED HER AND YES I THOUGHT OF HER ALL THE TIME BUT I HAD PASSED THE POINT OF NO RETURN SO WHY DWELL ON IT. HELL WITH HER AND HIM AND I HOPE THERE HAPPY CAUSE TONIGHT I WILL BE. TOMORROW I WILL START AGAIN. AS I SAT THERE ON MY STOOL IN A DARK CORNER OF THE BAR ALONE PEOPLE I KNEW KEPT

COMING UP AND SAYING HI AND HOW BAD THEY
FELT FOR ME CAUSE THEY KNEW WHAT A GREAT
GUY I WAS. HOW THEY DID NOT KNOW THAT THEY
WERE JUST FUELING MY CAUSE. EVERY TIME THEY
TOLD A GIRLFRIEND OF THEIRS HOW GREAT A GUY
I WAS THE MORE THEIR GIRLFRIEND WOULD WANT
ME, BUT I WAS NOT A GREAT GUY AT ALL. I WAS A
MONSTER. I WOULD END UP DANCING ALL NIGHT
OVER AND OVER GIRL AFTER GIRL AND AT THE
END OF THE NIGHT I WOULD HAVE TEN NUMBERS
AND A SECRET MEETING AT MY HOUSE. IF I DID
NOT GET A HOOK UP I WOULD JUST CALL ONE OF
THOSE GIRLS I WAS STRINGING ALONG. IN A
MONTHS TIME I PROBABLY SLEPT ALONE TEN
TIMES. IT WAS GREAT OR WAS IT. WAS I DECEIVING
MYSELF? WHAT TRICKERY HAD I USED TO FOOL
MY HEART INTO NOT LOVING OR FEELING. HELL I
EVEN CAUGHT SARAH STARTING TO LOOK AGAIN
BUT THAT WOULD BE POISONOUS. SHE COULD
MELT MY DEFENSES SO I STAYED CLEAR OF HER.
NEVER HOLDING A CONVERSATION AND NEVER
LOOKING TOO LONG. HOW COULD SOMETHING SO
BEAUTIFUL AS LOVE TURN OUT SOMETHING SO

113

UGLY. I WAS A GOOD LOOKING MAN BUT I FELT MY SOUL WAS UGLY. I WAS UGLY INSIDE AND I LIKED IT. HOW MANY MORE MONSTERS COULD I CREATE WITH MY MANIPULATION? WITH EMPTY PROMISES AND UNTRUE LOVES AND WORDS I WAS TURNING THEM FASTER THAN THE EYE COULD SEE. HOW CAN I STOP THE MONSTER INSIDE OF ME OR CAN ANYONE. IS THIS MY FATE? WHAT WILL BECOME OF MY SOUL. WILL I PERISH IN THE FIERY HELLS OR FALL TO MY OWN GREED. ONLY TIME CAN TELL.

Chapter 15

I Make A New Friend

I STARTED VISITING MY DADS WORK DURING MY LUNCH HOUR WHERE SEVERAL YOUNG LADIES WORKED. THEY WERE VERY PRETTY AND ONE WAS LIKE MY SISTER. HER NAME WAS AMY AND SHE WAS MY HEART. I LOVED HER AS A SISTER AND I STILL DO. SHE HELPED ME THROUGH A LOT OF HARD TIMES IN MY LIFE AND WAS ALWAYS THERE WHEN I NEEDED A RIDE AFTER A FEW TOO MANY SPIRITS AT THE LOCAL BAR. THERE WAS A NEW GIRL AT THIS VISIT AND HER NAME WAS MARIE AND SHE JUST STARTED WORKING THERE. OH SHE WAS VERY PRETTY AND I ASKED MY SISTER ABOUT HER. SHE TOLD ME SHE WAS SINGLE AND THAT I

SHOULD ASK HER OUT SO THAT IS WHAT I DID. WE WENT OUT TO LUNCH SEVERAL TIMES BUT SHE WOULD NOT EVEN LET ME GET CLOSE TO HER NO MATTER WHAT LINES I USED. SHE COULD SEE RIGHT THROUGH ME. SHE SAW THE MONSTER WITH IN AND STAYED WELL CLEAR. BEFORE YOU KNEW IT WE WERE GOING OUT AT NIGHT BUT ONLY AS FRIENDS AND I WOULD CONFIDE IN HER ABOUT THE GIRLS I HAD MET. WE HAD A BALL WHEN WE WERE TOGETHER. WE WOULD GOTO A FRIENDS HOUSE TOGETHER WERE THE BAND I WAS IN PRACTICED. SEVERAL TIMES WE WOULD STAY THE NIGHT AND WE WOULD SLEEP TOGETHER BUT SHE WOULD NOT LET ME DO NOTHING BUT HOLD HER. THEIR WAS NO KISSING EXCEPT ON HER CHEEK. EVERY MOVE I MADE WAS IMMEDIATELY SHUT DOWN. SHE SAW RIGHT THROUGH MY ACT BUT IT DID NOT MATTER I WAS HAPPY JUST BEING WITH HER. THE DRUMMER AND I MADE PLANS TO GOTO THE BEACH THE NEXT WEEKEND SO I ASKED HER IF SHE WOULD LIKE TO GO. TO MY SURPRISE SHE SAID YES. WHEN FRIDAY FINALLY ARRIVED WE MET AT MY DADS OFFICE AND ON THE ROAD WE ALL

117

WENT. WE FINALLY REACHED THE BEACH AROUND TWO AND A HALF HOURS LATER. THAT NIGHT WE GOT A COOLER FULL OF BEER AND SOME PEPPERMINT FLAVORED LIQUOR AND SAT AROUND THE POOL. WE DRANK AND TALKED ALL NIGHT OF PLAYING GIGS AROUND THE BEACH AREA. AS THE NIGHT PROGRESSED WE FOUND OURSELVES SITTING IN THE JACUZZI. SHE SAT RIGHT BESIDE ME AND I COULD FEEL THE FLESH OF HER LEG AGAINST MIND. THIS LITTLE TOUCH SET ME OFF. I COULD HAVE GRABBED HER AND MADE LOVE TO HER RIGHT THERE. SHE DROVE ME WILD INSIDE. EVERY THING ABOUT HER WAS PERFECT. LATER THAT NIGHT WE WENT UP TO THE ROOM AND GOT INTO THE LARGE KING SIZED BED. SHE WORE A T SHIRT AND PAJAMA BOTTOMS AND I WORE JUST MY BOXERS. AS WE LAID THERE TOGETHER I PULLED HER CLOSE TO ME AND HELD HER CLOSE TO ME. I WAS SO NERVOUS I COULD HEAR MY SELF BREATHE. THIS NIGHT WOULD BE DIFFERENT. SHE LET ME PASSED HER GUARD BUT ONLY SO FAR. I WOULD GENTLY RUB HER THIGH WITH MY FREE HAND AND MOVED UP TO THE FLATNESS OF HER

STOMACH. AS SOON AS I WENT JUST A LITTLE TO FAR SHE WOULD GRAB MY HAND AND PUT IT BACK IN AN APPROPRIATE PLACE. THAT IS AS FAR AS I GOT. I TRIED TO KISS HER ON THE LIPS AND JUST BEFORE OUR LIPS WOULD TOUCH SHED TURN HER HEAD SO MY LIPS WOULD MISS THEIR MARK AND LAND ON HER CHEEK. IT DID NOT MATTER TO ME THOUGH. DO NOT GET ME WRONG I WAS VERY EXCITED AND I KNOW SHE COULD FEEL IT AGAINST HER SIDE BUT IT WAS OK. FOR HER I FOUND MYSELF WANTING AND WILLING TO WAIT MORE AND MORE. I GENTLY PULLED HER LONG HAIR TO THE SIDE SO TO EXPOSE HER SLENDER NECK LINE. I GENTLY KISSED IT UP AND DOWN TO THE COLLOR OF HER SHIRT AND SHE THEN TURNED AWAY FROM ME ONTO HER SIDE. SHE BACKED HER BODY INTO MINE SO THAT WE FIT TOGETHER LIKE A PUZZLE. I COULD FEEL HER PUSH AGAINST MY MANHOOD SO I KNOW SHE WANTED ME JUST AS MUCH AS I WANTED HER BUT STILL SHE WOULD NOT LET ME ADVANCE. THAT WAS ONE OF THE LONGEST NIGHTS I HAVE EVER HAD FOR I LAID THERE ALL NIGHT HOLDING HER THINKING OFF HOW SWEET IT

119

WILL BE WHEN HE TIME COMES. MORNING FINALLY CAME AND TOOK HER OUT TO BREAKFAST WHERE WE GOSSIPED ABOUT THINGS GOING ON AT MY DADS OFFICE. WHO WAS SEEING WHO AND WHO DID WHAT? AFTER BREAKFAST WE HEADED TO THE BEACH WHERE WE LAID OUT IN THE SUN AND PLAYED IN THE SURF OF THE ATLANTIC. IT WAS A PERFECT DAY IF I HAD EVER PICTURED ONE. WE WRESTLED IN THE WATER AND WE LAID THERE AND TALKED. WE WENT WALKING DOWN THE BEACH WERE WE LOOKED FOR SHELLS SCATTERED ACROSS WHERE THE WATER TOUCHED THE SAND. BEFORE YOU KNEW IT THE SUN WAS SETTING AND WE HAD FOUND OURSELVES A MILE DOWN THE BEACH FROM OUR MOTEL SO WE TURNED AROUND AND HEADED BACK. THE NIGHT WENT JUST LIKE THE NIGHT BEFORE. SHE LET ME HOLD HER , KISS HER NECK BUT THAT WAS ABOUT IT. NOT EVEN A KISS. ON THE LIPS. SHE WAS SO CLOSE BUT OH SO DISTANT. SHE GUARDED HER HEART LIKE NO ONE I HAD EVER SEEN. THE NEXT MORNING WE AWOKE AND ATE BREAKFAST AGAIN AND HEADED BACK HOME. WE PULLED INTO HER DRIVE AND I LET HER

OUT ONLY TO FIND MYSELF AT MY FRIENDS HOUSE
THE NEXT NIGHT FOR BAND PRACTICE AND, YUP,
SHE WAS THERE.

Chapter 16

The Rest of the Story

I GUESS I NEVER THOUGHT OF THE REST OF THE STORY OF FRANKENSTEIN. SEE AT THE END THEY MADE A MISS FRANKENSTEIN AND HE DID HAVE A HEART. THAT WAS HIS ONE WEAKNESS. HE HAD A GOOD HEART AND NO MATTER HOW BAD I WAS I STILL HAD A GOOD HEART. NO MATTER HOW HARD I WOULD TRY TO BE SOMETHING I WAS NOT. I WAS STILL JUST A GOOD MAN NO MATTER WHAT I DID. DAY AFTER DAY ME AND MARIE WOULD EAT AND HANG OUT TOGETHER AND EVERY DAY THE CLOSER I WOULD GET TO HER. SHE WOULD ONLY LET ME GET SO FAR BUT STILL I CAME BACK TIME AND TIME AGAIN. WHAT COMPELLED ME TOO HER. WE HAVE NOT EVEN HAD SEX YET STILL IM HERE TOTALLY INFATUATED WITH HER. IT MAKES NO

SENSE TO ME. IM IN LOVE WITH HER AND I DO NOT KNOW WHY. WHEN WERE APART I THINK OF HER CONSTANTLY AND FIND MYSELF WANTING TO BE NEAR HER. I SEE IT IN HER EYES THAT SHE THINKS OF ME TOO. IS THIS WHAT IS TO BECOME OF ME? IS ALL THIS SOME WEIRDED OUT TEST? FATE IS A CRAZY THING I KNOW. WHEN SHE LOOKS AT ME I CAN FEEL A LOVE GROWING FROM WITHIN HER FOR ME TOO. I CAN FEEL IT IN HER TOUCH. I CAN HEAR IT IN THE NERVOUSNESS OF HER VOICE. EVERY TIME MY PHONE RINGS I WATCH HER GLANCE OVER TO SEE WHO IS CALLING ME. ONCE SHE EVEN GOT MAD AND SAID SHE HATED MY PHONE. SOMETIMES A MONSTER CAN BE TURNED INTO SOMETHING BEAUTIFUL. KINDA LIKE THE UGLY DUCKLING STORY WE HEARD AS A CHILD. I SIT HERE AND GO THROUGH ALL MY PAST RELATIONSHIPS POINTING ON EVERY MISTAKE I MADE AND LOOK AT EVERY TIME I COULD HAVE DONE SOMETHING BETTER. SHE HAS REVIVED MY DECAYING HEART. A NEW BREATHE HAS BEEN BREATHED IN AND I FEEL ALIVE AGAIN. LORD PLEASE LET THIS ONE WORK OUT. AND FOR MARIE

AS YOU LIE THERE AWAKE IN YOUR BED TONIGHT KNOW THAT I AM THINKING OF YOU AND IN MY ARMS IM HOLDING YOU TIGHT. I HOPE YOU CAN FEEL MY LIPS AGAINST THE FLESH OF YOUR NECK AND IMAGINE THE TASTE OF MY KISS ON YOUR LIPS FOR HOPEFULLY SOON IT WILL HAPPEN. I HAVE FOUND A NEW ME AND I THINK I LIKE HIM. HE SEEMS TO BE A VERY DIFFERENT GUY THAN WHAT I TRIED TO MAKE HIM. NO MATTER HOW MUCH WE TRY TO BE SOMETHING WE'RE NOT WE WILL ALWAYS END UP JUST WHO WE ARE. SO TONIGHT AS YOU GET READY TO GO OUT ON THE TOWN OR WHILE YOU'RE LYING IN YOUR LONELY BED, JUST THINK LOVE CAN BE RIGHT AROUND THE CORNER. NEVER GIVE UP ON LOVE FOR NO MATTER HOW MUCH YOU TRY TO HIDE FROM AND RUN FROM IT, IT WILL FIND AND CATCH YOU AND LEAVE YOU WANTING. HAVE FAITH. IT'S OUT THERE SOMEWHERE AND THE WORLD REALLY IS NOT AS BIG AS IT SEEMS. SOMETIMES YOU JUST GOT TO OPEN YOUR EYES AND WAIT FOR THE WORLD TO CATCH UP WITH YOU.

www.ingramcontent.com/pod-product-compliance
Lightning Source LLC
Chambersburg PA
CBHW051428280526
45785CB00003B/1200